THE BANKER'S GUIDE TO INVESTMENT BANKING

Securities & Underwriting Activities in Commercial Banking

THE BANKER'S GUIDE TO INVESTMENT BANKING

Securities & Underwriting Activities in Commercial Banking

Hazel J. Johnson, Ph.D., C.P.A
University of Louisville
College of Business and Public Administration

IRWIN
Professional Publishing®

Chicago • London • Singapore

A Bankline Publication

IRWIN
Professional Publishing®

©Richard D. Irwin, A Times Mirror Higher Education Group, Inc. company, 1996

▼▼ Times Mirror
M Higher Education Group

Library of Congress Cataloging-in-Publication Data

Johnson, Hazel J.
    Bankers' guide to investment banking: securities & under-
writing activities in commercial banking / Hazel J. Johnson.
        p.   cm. -- (A bankline publication)
    Includes index.
    ISBN 1-55738-747-8
    1. Investment banking—United States. I. Title. II. Series.
HG4930.5.J84   1996
    332.66—dc2   96–3744

Printed in the United States of America
1 2 3 4 5 6 7 8 9 0 B S 3 2 1 0 9 8 7 6

In loving memory of
Ida W. Kelly and Lucille V. Johnson

PREFACE

It is clear to all observers of the commercial banking industry that increased fee income and other noninterest revenues are essential for the future viability of the industry. Investment banking activities are part of an increasingly wider array of services offered by commercial banks. In the future, as Glass-Steagall barriers continue to erode or are completely dismantled, expansion of these activities is inevitable.

The demand for financing in capital markets will intensify in the future. Corporate issuers prefer flexibility beyond traditional bank lending and increasingly will be able to obtain it. Internationally, enterprises that have been operated by governments will continue to be privatized, requiring large amounts of capital. As pension funds grow in developed and developing countries, this capital increasingly will become available. Trends in corporate finance, privatization, and pension fund development all suggest strong future growth in capital markets activity. U.S. commercial banks will be affected by all these trends; at the same time, margins in traditional commercial lending will be under continuing pressure because of competitive forces. These forces will encourage commercial bankers to continue to enter the securities arena. The commercial bank that elects not to do so may relegate itself to the passive position of allowing its competition to decide its fate.

Actually, securities underwriting is closely related to bank loan syndication. An investment banker must have established a relationship with the issuing client, win the mandate to manage a new securities issue, and form an underwriting syndicate. In loan syndications, a commercial lending officer also must have a strong client relationship to manage the financing and must assemble a group of banks (a syndicate). In securities underwriting, the funding is provided by the investing public. In a loan syndication, the funding is provided by participating banks. Successful securities underwriters have both (1) a strong perception of their clients' capabilities and financial position and (2) a keen awareness of market conditions. The skills of successful loan syndication can be enhanced and transferred to the investment banking arena. Perhaps the most successful underwriting teams that can be formed within a commercial bank consist of the commercial lenders and securities trading officers.

The involvement of commercial banks in investment banking is a natural outgrowth. Banks have a competitive advantage in credit analysis, large capital bases, and significant placing power through existing clients (if this resource is developed). When commercial banking and investment banking are once again allowed to develop in an unencumbered, pre-Glass-Steagall sense, both industries will thrive. As a direct result, improved financing alternatives will facilitate continued economic growth for the United States.

Hazel J. Johnson, Ph.D., C.P.A.

CONTENTS

CHAPTER 1

Participating in the Securities Industry   1

Introduction   1
Investment Banking Defined   2
The Glass-Steagall Act   3
Relaxation of the Glass-Steagall Barrier   4
Other Legislation Affecting Investment Banking Powers   6
    The National Bank Act   6
    The Bank Holding Company Act   6
Dismantling Investment Banking Restrictions   7
A Matter of Necessity   8
A New Breed of Banker?   10
    Volatility for J. P. Morgan   10
    An Uncertain Future for Bankers Trust   11
The Right Mix   12
Selected References   13
Endnotes   13

CHAPTER 2

Underwriting Activities   15

Introduction   15
Winning the Mandate   16
Advising Clients   20
    Debt versus Equity   20
    Floating versus Fixed-Rate Debt   24
    Using Derivatives to Manage Interest Rate Risk   26
    Public versus Private Placement   00
The Public Offering   34
    The Lead Manager   35
    The Syndicate   37

The Successful Underwriting   41
Selected References   42
Endnotes   42

CHAPTER 3

Underwriting of Treasury and Municipal Bonds   43

Introduction   43
Underwriting Powers of Commercial Banks   44
Treasury Securities   48
    Characteristics of Treasury Securities   48
    The Primary Market for Treasuries   50
    The Auction Process   52
    Primary Government Securities Dealers   55
Municipal Bonds   58
    Municipal Bonds and the Tax Reform Act of 1986   59
    The Underwriting Process   61
    Underwriters' Disclosure Responsibilities   62
    Issues to Be Addressed as an Underwriter   67
    Insured Municipal Bonds   70
Very Different Markets   72
Selected References   73
Endnotes   73

CHAPTER 4

The Section 20 Subsidiary   75

Introduction   75
Powers of Section 20 Subsidiaries   77
    Authorized Subsidiaries   77
    The Toronto-Dominion Case   80
Underwriting Stocks   83
    Preferred Stock   84
    Common Stock   85
    Exchange Listing of Common Stock   87
Underwriting Corporate Bonds   97
    Types of Bonds   100
    Bond Ratings   105

Underwriting Municipal Revenue Bonds   107
    Electric Utility Bonds   107
    Other Issuers   109
The Need for Industry Expertise   109
Selected References   110
Endnotes   110

CHAPTER 5

Asset-Backed Securities   113

Introduction   113
The Nature of Asset-Backed Securities   114
    Pass-Through Securities   114
    Asset-Backed Bonds   115
    Pay-Through Bonds   115
    A Comparison   116
The Benefits and Costs of Securitization   119
Basic Elements of a Securitization   120
Evaluating and Controlling Credit Risk   124
    The Asset Pool   125
    The Originator   129
    The Servicer   132
    The Issuer   134
    The Trustee   137
    Credit Enhancement   137
Mortgage-Backed Pass-Through Securities   140
Mortgage-Backed Pay-Through Bonds   143
The Direction of the Industry   146
Selected References   148
Endnotes   148

CHAPTER 6

Future Trends in Commercial and Investment Banking   149

Introduction   149
Profits and Investment Banking   150

The Case of Goldman Sachs   153
Investment Banking Corporate Culture   157
        Citicorp   157
        J. P. Morgan   159
The Movement Toward Fund Management   162
        PNC Mutual Funds   162
        Mellon Bank, the Boston Co., and Dreyfus Corporation   164
Private Equity Issues   166
International Connections   169
        Deutsche Bank   169
        NationsBank   171
        The Transformation   173
        Selected References   175
        Endnotes   175

APPENDIX
PRESENT AND FUTURE VALUE TABLES   177

A–1
Future Value of $1   178

A–2
Future Value of an Annuity of $1   181

A–3
Present Value of $1   184

A–4
Present Value of an Annuity of $1   187

INDEX   191

CHAPTER 1

Participating in the Securities Industry

INTRODUCTION

Since 1933, commercial banks in the United States have been precluded by federal law from engaging in securities activities. The Glass-Steagall Act separated commercial banking from investment banking.

Beginning in the late 1980s, however, this barrier has been eroded. Banks long have been permitted to engage in the underwriting of government securities and certain municipal securities. By special permission of the Federal Reserve, a small number of banks now operate so-called Section 20 subsidiaries. Offshore, U.S. commercial banks have begun to make their presence felt in underwriting syndicates. Domestically, serious debate continues to chip away Glass-Steagall barriers. There is no doubt that U.S. commercial banks now have the capital to engage in the primarily fee-driven activity of investment banking. Clearly commercial banks must turn increasingly to lines of business that supplement shrinking lending margins.

At the same time, legislative hurdles are not the only barriers to be overcome. The cultural differences between commercial and investment banking must be reconciled. The 60-year separation of commercial and investment banks has left some institutions less prepared to participate in what is undoubtedly one of the major growth fields in financial services.

INVESTMENT BANKING DEFINED

An investment banker is a financial intermediary that is instrumental in the sale and distribution of newly issued securities. The investment banker purchases securities from the issuer, as principal, and assumes the risk of distribution to ultimate investors. This process is referred to as *underwriting*. To diversify the risk associated with underwriting new securities, investment bankers frequently form syndicates—groups of investment bankers that share the risks. Each member of the syndicate agrees to sell a certain portion of the new issue. The difference between the price guaranteed to the issuer and the price at which the securities are sold to the investing public is the *underwriter's spread*.

A *firm commitment* represents the greatest risk that an investment banker can assume. In such an arrangement, the underwriter assumes 100 percent of the risk, to be shared with the syndicate, and agrees to purchase 100 percent of the offering. A *standby underwriting* is a commitment by the underwriter and the underwriting syndicate to purchase any securities that are not purchased by shareholders in connection with a rights offering. In a rights offering, existing shareholders may exercise a preemptive right to maintain their proportional ownership of the firm when new shares are issued. The rights offering frequently is associated with a lower-than-market price for the shares and, typically, expires after a specified date. A standby underwriting assures the issuing firm that any shares not purchased by existing shareholders will be purchased by the underwriting syndicate and subsequently sold to investors or held in the accounts of the syndicate members.

In a *best efforts* arrangement, an investment banker is essentially an agent. The underwriting syndicate agrees to sell whatever quantity of securities is placed with the public, but makes no guarantees as to the quantity ultimately to be sold. In some cases, the issuing firm may establish a minimum amount that it expects to be sold in connection with the new issue. Firms use the best efforts arrangement most often in the over-the-counter market for initial public offerings (IPOs). Established firms are more likely to enter into underwriting arrangements that contain a firm commitment.

These are the basic functions of an investment banker. The actual implementation of investment banking activities, however, is quite varied and often industry specific. For example, there are significant differences between investment banking activities in bond and stock markets. There are also differences between the issuance of government bonds and corporate bonds. Some of the competitive advantages of U.S. commercial banks in new-issue markets are directly related to the Glass-Steagall limitations of banks to a narrowly defined range of investment banking activities.

THE GLASS-STEAGALL ACT

The Banking Act of 1933 represented major legislative reform of the U.S. banking system at the federal level. This act (and the Banking Act of 1935) created the Federal Deposit Insurance Corporation (FDIC) and the Federal Open Market Committee. Control of monetary policy was placed in the hands of the Federal Reserve Board of Governors. In addition, sections 16, 20, 21, and 32 separated the commercial banking and investment banking industries in what is commonly referred to as the Glass-Steagall Act.

- Section 16 prohibits Federal Reserve member banks from owning equity securities. This section also prohibits member banks from underwriting and dealing in any securities with the exception of U.S. Treasury securities, federal agency securities, and general obligation securities of states and municipal governments.

- Section 20 prohibits Federal Reserve member banks from affiliating with firms engaged principally in underwriting and selling corporate bonds and equity securities.
- Section 21 targets securities firms, specifically underwriters of corporate securities. Such institutions may not accept deposits.
- Section 32 separates the control of banks and securities firms. This section forbids interlocking directorates between member banks and securities firms.

Thus, since Glass-Steagall, U.S. banks have been restricted with respect to investment banking activities. Passage of the act caused commercial banks that offered investment banking services to divest themselves of such affiliates. Although Glass-Steagall permitted Federal Reserve member banks to buy and sell securities without recourse as agents for their customers, subsequent rulings by the comptroller of the currency prohibited commercial banks from engaging in any brokerage activities.

RELAXATION OF THE GLASS-STEAGALL BARRIER

The Glass-Steagall Act has not been repealed; however, U.S. bank regulators have granted expanded powers with respect to securities activities. During the 1980s, commercial banks obtained permission from the Federal Reserve Board to:

- Underwrite limited amounts of asset-backed securities, corporate bonds, and commercial paper through bank holding company affiliates.
- Act as investment advisors to corporate clients.

- Sponsor mutual fund issues.
- Offer discount brokerage services.

Beginning in 1987, the Federal Reserve interpreted the Glass-Steagall Act in a way that permits banks to engage indirectly in securities activities. Section 20 of the Glass-Steagall Act prohibits Federal Reserve member banks from affiliating with any organization "engaged principally" in the issue, flotation, underwriting, public sale or distribution of securities. The Federal Reserve interpreted Section 20 as permitting a bank to affiliate with a firm engaged in securities transactions, as long as securities transactions are not the principal business of the affiliate. The 1987 ruling by the Federal Reserve allowed bank securities affiliates to underwrite commercial paper, revenue bonds, and other securities. The U.S. Supreme Court upheld this ruling in 1988 when challenged in federal court by securities broker-dealers. The Section 20 subsidiaries, thus, could underwrite and deal in corporate debt securities to the extent that these activities did not generate more than 10 percent of the total underwriting volume for the securities affiliate.

The Federal Reserve ruling has since been expanded. Now Section 20 subsidiaries can underwrite and deal in:

- Municipal revenue bonds.
- Mortgage-related securities.
- Commercial paper.
- Asset-backed securities (in addition to mortgage-related securities).
- Corporate debt.
- Corporate equity.

Chapter 3 provides an analysis of the underwriting powers granted by Glass-Steagall with respect to government and municipal bonds. Chapter 4 examines the exercise of powers under a Section 20 subsidiary. Chapter 5 examines the rapidly expanding market of asset-backed securities.

OTHER LEGISLATION AFFECTING INVESTMENT BANKING POWERS

The National Bank Act of 1863 addressed permissible powers for banks chartered by the comptroller of the currency. The Bank Holding Company Act of 1956 established the criteria under which nonbanking activities would be permitted.

The National Bank Act

The National Bank Act created the office of the comptroller of the currency and the national bank charter. This act permitted national banks to:

1. Accept general deposits.
2. Lend money on personal securities and make loans secured by real estate.
3. Discount and negotiate promissory notes, drafts, bills of exchange, and other evidences of debt.

The act also gave banks *incidental powers* that can change as methods of banking change over time. These incidental powers are conferred as necessary to "carry out the business of banking." Incidental powers have been interpreted by U.S. courts to include those activities convenient or useful to the performance of one of the established banking activities. Activities permitted under this "incidental powers" provision include leasing personal property and issuing letters of credit.

The Bank Holding Company Act

The ability of commercial banks to underwrite securities, or act as investment bankers, also is governed by the Bank Holding Company Act of 1956 and its amendments in 1970. According to this act, the Federal Reserve Board must determine which activities are permissible for bank holding companies. To establish a nonbank activity as permissible, either by regulation or by order, the activity must be shown to be "so closely related to banking or managing or controlling banks as to be a proper incident thereto." In reaching this conclusion, the Federal Reserve must consider whether:

- Banks engage in the proposed activity.
- Banks generally provide services so operationally or functionally similar to the proposed activity that they derive a competitive advantage for the proposed activity.
- Banks generally provide services so closely related to the proposed activity that they are essentially required to provide the proposed activity.

In applying the "proper incident" test, the Federal Reserve also must examine whether the activity of the bank holding company has benefits for the public. These benefits may include greater convenience, increased competition, and gains in efficiency that outweigh possible adverse effects, such as undue concentration, diminished competition, conflicts of interest, and unsound banking practices. Together, the Glass-Steagall Act, the National Bank Act, and the Bank Holding Company Act comprise both the permission and the constraints for commercial banks to participate in the securities industry. Recently, there have been renewed efforts to remove the remaining restrictions of commercial banks in the area of investment banking.

DISMANTLING INVESTMENT BANKING RESTRICTIONS

In 1995, the debate over dismantling Glass-Steagall restrictions for the combination of commercial banking and investment banking continued. The legislative remedies that were suggested originated from the U.S. House of Representatives, the U.S. Senate, and the Clinton administration.

The House Banking Committee proposed the establishment of securities subsidiaries that would be overseen by the Federal Reserve. For the first time, financial services holding companies would be permitted, replacing bank holding companies. Under this structure, a financial services holding company could own both commercial bank affiliates and investment bank affiliates.[1]

The U.S. Senate version of reform was much more far-reaching. This view of deregulation permitted banks to affiliate with companies of any kind. The central theme was that securities firms and insurance companies affiliated with banks would be regulated by the same regulators as their unaffiliated competitors. This version of the proposed reform relied primarily on existing statutory and regulatory restrictions on transactions between a bank and its affiliates to ensure that the bank is neither exerting an unfair competitive advantage nor being exploited.

The administration's proposal was similar to the House version. It not only included the financial services holding company but also permitted the introduction of an insurance affiliate.

Ultimately, the House Banking Committee version of reform went forward with certain modifications. The need for a separate subsidiary for securities activities was not, in all cases, maintained. To permit legislation that repeals Glass-Steagall to move forward, many contentious issues with respect to insurance powers and deregulation were placed in separate bills. The debate continues. Final legislation has not yet been passed. However, activity by commercial banks or financial services holding companies is clearly increasing in the investment banking field.

A MATTER OF NECESSITY

The movement of commercial banks into investment banking is not a luxury. It is a necessity. From 1983 to 1993, the volume of new commercial loans increased from $404 billion to $443 billion, an annual compound rate of increase of less than 1 percent. Over the same decade, new commercial paper issues grew from $184 billion to $554 billion, an increase of almost 12 percent per year. In addition, corporate bond issues rose over the same 10-year period from $643 billion to $2.27 trillion, a 13 percent annual increase. To survive, commercial bankers must become investment bankers. Many U.S. banks already have made significant strides in diversifying their income sources to include investment banking activities:

- J. P. Morgan & Company, as recently as 1987, generated noninterest revenue of only $1.4 billion while interest revenue amounted to $5.9 billion. By 1993, these relationships were completely reversed; securities activities generated $4.5 billion, while interest income was down to $1.7 billion.
- In 1993, Bankers Trust earned 50 percent of its net income from trading activities and another 25 percent to 30 percent from structuring derivatives for its clients.[2]
- Chase Manhattan has added hundreds of investment bankers and traders to its staff and invested nearly $100 million in constructing high-technology trading floors that facilitate communication between clients and traders.[3]

These activities are not limited to New York money-center banks. For example, through its Section 20 subsidiary, NationsBank now underwrites $15 billion in corporate bonds each year. Also, First Union has launched an aggressive campaign to attract corporate clients in need of all forms of finance.

Indeed, the provision of investment banking services is an extremely attractive field. Several U.S. institutions have completely revised their corporate culture to compete with investment banking firms such as Goldman Sachs and Lehman Brothers. In this evolution into commercial/investment banks, however, U.S. banks must be mindful of certain caveats along the way. J. P. Morgan and Bankers Trust provide useful examples.

A NEW BREED OF BANKER?

Volatility for J. P. Morgan

In 1933, J. P. Morgan was an elite investment banking operation. The passage of Glass-Steagall required divestiture of the investment banking operation. At the time, the 1933 legislation was thought to be a temporary condition. J. P. Morgan elected to retain its commercial bank charter to avoid having to build that infrastructure once the "temporary" legislation had been repealed. Finally, in the 1980s, when the Glass-Steagall barriers began to fall, J. P. Morgan was among the first to take advantage of special investment banking privileges. Today, J. P. Morgan is considered a global merchant bank. Ironically, its archrival in this race for recognition as a world-class investment bank is Bankers Trust. Both of these institutions have been adversely effected by recent developments in the securities field.

In 1994, 75 percent of J. P. Morgan's revenues were derived from new lines of business such as underwriting and securities trading, despite the fact that trading and risk-management operations were much less profitable in 1994 than in previous years. Morgan maintains a strong revenue stream from merger-and-acquisition advisory services and debt underwriting. The bank was given the authority to underwrite corporate stock in 1990. However, this market has proved to be more difficult to develop. Recent market setbacks (net income declined by 23 percent in 1994) have resulted in a downgrading of the bank's credit rating and a 5 percent staff reduction to trim overhead expenses.

Nevertheless, J. P. Morgan is well poised to be the first U.S. bank to successfully capture the title and capabilities of a global investment bank. Part of the reason for this strong potential is the firm's attention to relationship banking. J. P. Morgan developed this capability before the 1933 passage of the Glass-Steagall Act and has made it a tradition of the institution. Such emphasis on client relationships will sustain J. P. Morgan's profitability through the necessarily volatile movements of securities markets.

An Uncertain Future for Bankers Trust

Bankers Trust originally did not intend to become an investment bank; the firm has had a more entrepreneurial culture. In this sense, it has been compared to Citibank, with one important difference. Citibank has built a very strong retail base of operation, while Bankers Trust was forced to exit retail banking beginning in 1978. The institution defined itself as a collection of entrepreneurs who were rewarded for developing new products and businesses. At first it would be a wholesale bank and evolve into a world-class merchant and investment bank.

As the leveraged buyout boom of the 1980s subsided, this group of entrepreneurs, led by Charles Sanford, Jr., turned their attention to the risk-management business, that is, derivatives. The trading expertise of Bankers Trust personnel and its preeminence in sophisticated derivatives resulted in $1 billion in profits for both 1992 and 1993. Then, trading losses associated with rising interest rates and slumping derivatives sales associated with client losses caused profits to decline significantly. Much publicized losses and legal proceedings with Procter & Gamble Company and Gibson Greeting Cards hurt both profits and public perception. Bankers Trust did not (or could not) diversify to protect itself from market volatility. Its overemphasis in one area caused an overexposure. Profits in 1994 sank by 38 percent as compared to 1993 results.

The emphasis on short-term, proprietary trading hurt the bank's relationships with its clients. Now, the bank faces significant challenges in rebuilding that confidence.

To add to the already daunting task of rebuilding client confidence and constructing a broader base of financial services, Bankers Trust faces a leadership crisis. The institution's first-quarter loss of $157 million in 1995 generated a rash of resignations. Among these are

- Business manager, individual services group.
- Head of global finance sales.
- Head of mergers and acquisitions.

- Head of emerging markets.
- Chief financial officer (effective in 1996).
- Charles Sanford, Jr., chairman and chief executive officer (effective in 1996).

A troubling question now is whether Bankers Trust can remain an independent institution.

Signaling a new direction for the institution has been the appointment of the new chairman and CEO. Frank N. Newman, former deputy Treasury secretary and former chief financial officer of BankAmerica and Wells Fargo & Co., assumed the responsibilities of Bankers Trust CEO beginning January 1, 1996, and will assume the responsibilities of chairman on April 1 of the same year. This appointment was unexpected because Eugene Shanks, the president who served Sanford and presided over the bank's ascendancy in the derivatives market, had been considered the likely successor to Sanford. The appointment of Newman underscored the intention of the bank to move toward a more client-centered focus.

The experience of Bankers Trust illustrates an important lesson for the commercial banking industry. A commercial bank should not forsake its roots as a provider of financial services and become a highly specialized house with only one or two products. It is entirely counterproductive to move from one environment in which a narrowly defined line of products may be offered (loans and deposits) into a new environment in which, again, only a narrowly defined range of products may be offered (derivatives, for example).

THE RIGHT MIX

For commercial banks, participating in the securities industry is a vital step in remaining a competitive force in financial services. This activity should be blended with the traditional services offered by commercial banks. Each institution should analyze its own strengths to offer the correct form of investment banking service. The key is to use investment banking powers to properly diversify the institution's portfolio of services.

SELECTED REFERENCES

Fitch, Thomas. *Dictionary of Banking Terms*. Hauppauge, NY: Barron's Educational Series, 1990.

Holland, Kelley. "Brain Drain at Bankers Trust." *Business Week*, July 10, 1995, p. 36.

Pavel, Christine A. *Securitization: The Analysis and Development of the Loan-Based/Asset-Backed Securities Markets*. Chicago: Probus Publishing Company, 1989.

Rogers, David. *The Future of American Banking: Managing for Change*. New York: McGraw-Hill, 1993.

Sprong, Kenneth. *Banking Regulation: Its Purposes, Implementation, and Effects*. 3rd ed. Kansas City: Federal Reserve Bank of Kansas City, Division of Supervision and Structure, 1990.

The Wall Street Journal, various issues.

ENDNOTES

1. This concept is very similar to that adopted in Mexico where a holding company may own a bank, a securities firm, and an insurance affiliate.

2. Because of the highly publicized financial losses of Procter & Gamble Company and Gibson Greeting Cards, Bankers Trust has come under increasing pressure as a result of its derivatives activities.

3. This capability in capital markets was undoubtedly one of the attractions for Chemical Banking when Chase and Chemical merged in mid-1995.

CHAPTER 2

Underwriting Activities

INTRODUCTION

A number of activities are appropriate for an investment banker, including securities underwriting, secondary market trading, secondary market making, corporate restructuring, financial engineering (zero-coupon securities, mortgage-backed securities, other asset-backed securities, and derivatives), merchant banking, and investment management. However, for commercial banks, the activities that have been most restricted are those associated with corporate securities underwriting.

Ironically, securities underwriting is closely related to loan syndication. The investment banker must have established a relationship with the issuing client and win the mandate to manage the issue. The lead manager of a new issue must walk a thin line between advocacy for the client and objective evaluation. In loan syndications, the funding is provided by the financial institution or a group of financial institutions (a syndicate). In securities underwriting, the funding is provided by the investing public. The functions that are most different from a traditional loan syndication are the required disclosures associated with a public offer and, to a lesser extent, the coordination of the underwriting syndicate. Nevertheless, the skills of successful loan syndication can be enhanced and transferred to the investment banking arena.

WINNING THE MANDATE

Commercial bankers comfortable with the practice of relationship banking can be successful in obtaining the engagement to manage a securities underwriting; that is, winning the mandate. Every competent commercial loan officer has mastered the skills of assessing the financial position of a client and evaluating the probable success of a potential commercial loan. These skills transfer directly into investment banking. An investment banker must be able to evaluate the creditworthiness of a client and its prospects for success.

In investment banking, however, market conditions unrelated to the prospective securities issuer also must be assessed. The loan will not be held in the bank's own account. Instead, the client will issue a security to be purchased by the investing public and later traded in secondary markets. As a result, market conditions at the time of issue must be fully understood.

The successful investment banker provides its client with dependable and up-to-date information about market conditions. This necessarily requires that the investment banker have a total commitment (on a full-time basis) to assessing primary market conditions. Admittedly, this is a significant resource allocation for a small- or medium-size commercial bank. At the same time, a commercial bank with a small dedicated investment banking team can have an advantage over larger firms. It is sometimes said that major investment banking firms send their most experienced bankers to make presentations that will result in winning a mandate. Once the engagement is secure, less experienced bankers actually manage the transaction. Thus, a smaller institution can gain a competitive advantage by offering a higher level of service until the transaction is completed.

Also, smaller investment banks may be the only type of firm through which a medium-size issuer can hope to float a public issue. The largest, most established investment bankers are not as likely to take on a smaller client. Investment banking fees are based on the size of the securities issue—smaller issues result in smaller fees. More established investment banks seek larger transactions and bypass the smaller issues. These smaller issues represent perhaps the greatest opportunity for the medium-size commercial bank to enter the field of investment banking.

Basic elements of understanding the client's position and market conditions are

- *Understanding the client's strategic and operational plans.* An investment banker must understand its client's financial goals and legal constraints. To be effective in this effort, the client must be forthcoming with all information relative to its current plans and future prospects.

- *Determining whether the client is attempting to actively manage the right-hand side of its balance sheet.* Does the client intend to take advantage of changing market conditions? When interest rates and other economic factors fluctuate, does the client intend to adjust its funding base? Or, alternatively, does the client intend to establish a long-term capital structure that will remain essentially stable? The answers to these questions depend not only on the stated intentions of the client but also on the management resources of the client. Without an active asset-liability management function, the client firm is less able to quickly react to changing market conditions.

- *Being prepared to offer liability management advice.* A smaller issuing firm necessarily depends more on its investment banker. Therefore, the successful investment banker must be prepared to offer advice

and support for managing the public issue and subsequent financings. In essence, winning the mandate may depend on being able to demonstrate that
ongoing support and advice will be available.

- *Being prepared to assist with credit rating issues.*
  When client firms have credit ratings that are less
  than AAA, presenting a debt issue to credit rating
  agencies is critical. The successful investment
  banker demonstrates willingness and ability to present the issue to credit rating agencies in clear and
  objective terms that provide all necessary information for a correct rating.

- *Contemplating the aftermarket.* The performance of
  debt and equity issues in the secondary market has
  a direct bearing on the ability of the issuer to
  approach the capital markets again at a later date.
  The issues of secondary trading should be broached
  by the investment banker during a presentation so
  that the client firm realizes that the investment
  banker is interested in the long-term position of
  the client firm. In some cases, the investment
  banker may make a market in the securities to be
  issued. In other cases, this function is performed
  by other financial institutions. In any event, the
  successful investment banker must be attentive to
  this issue.

- *Relationship banking.* A commercial bank/invest-
  ment bank has a competitive advantage when working with client firms with which it already has a
  relationship. The informational advantage is that
  past financial data is available, as well as past payment history. Most often, trust also has been established. On the other hand, presenting a proposal to
  a firm that has a primary banking relationship with
  another institution creates a different set of circumstances. When the bank with which the potential
  client has an established relationship does not have
  an investment banking function, the potential client

is unlikely to feel hesitancy or conflict because there is no established investment banking relationship with the other institution. Making a presentation to a potential client who has a primary banking relationship with an institution that has an investment banking affiliate is considerably more difficult. Here the presenting institution must assert tactfully that it can provide better service and a superior ongoing relationship.

- *Addressing the competitive issues.* Although relationships are critical, ultimately the successful investment banker wins the mandate, and subsequent mandates, because it provides high-quality service and charges competitive fees. A competitive fee schedule can be established only when the investment banking function has been structured to be as efficient as any other function of the bank.

Once a relationship has been established with an investment bank, issuing firms typically continue to use the services of that investment bank. As part of this relationship, the services rendered include issuance (including advice for structuring), the underwriting process, and distribution of the new securities. Possibly one or more of these functions can be assigned to different firms. Then, all necessary steps and approvals for issuance may be handled by one investment bank, while actual underwriting and distribution are assigned to other firms. The separation of these functions depends on the capabilities of the investment bank and, more recently, on whether the issue is a regular registration or a shelf registration with the Securities and Exchange Commission. The principal activities of the investment banker that wins the mandate are

- Advising the client on the structure of the issue.
- Negotiating the terms of the underwriting and forming the syndicate.
- Managing the distribution process.

ADVISING CLIENTS

The primary areas for advising clients about new issues of securities are the actual structure of the issue, the timing of the issue, and whether a public or private placement is preferable. Questions related to the structure of the issue focus on whether debt or equity should be used and, if debt is preferable, whether the issue should be fixed rate and whether it should be short- or long-term. The primary timing consideration involves plans for future issues and desired flexibility. Whether an issue should be a public or private placement depends on cost considerations and the type of issue.

Debt versus Equity

Generally, *debt* issues produce a superior cash flow stream for the issuing firm as compared to equity. There are two reasons for this generalization.

1. The rate of return that investors in debt securities require is generally lower than the rate of return required by equity investors.
2. Interest payments associated with the debt issue are tax deductible, while dividend payments on equity are not.

At the same time, the ability of a firm to issue debt depends on its *debt capacity.* Commercial bankers bring a competitive advantage to the investment banking field in that commercial loan officers traditionally are well versed in assessing a firm's debt capacity. The commercial bank credit analysis function is one that prepares investment bankers to measure the ability of a client to meet interest payments and to retire debt. Specific ratios helpful in this regard are the debt ratio, the times-interest-earned ratio, and the fixed-charge-coverage ratio.

The *debt ratio* is the percentage of a firm's assets that is financed with debt.

$$DR = \frac{\text{Debt}}{\text{Total Assets}} \qquad (1)$$

If the debt ratio is high by industry standards or by other comparisons, a large debt issue by the firm may not be advisable. At a minimum, a high debt ratio raises the cost of additional debt issues in the marketplace. At worst, a debt issue does not attract adequate interest and is not fully subscribed. The use of debt is commonly referred to as *leverage*. Undue leverage causes the cost of capital to rise to unacceptable levels and the underwriting is not successful.

The times-interest-earned ratio is not based on the balance sheet of the client firm, instead, it is a measure of the firm's ability to meet interest payments.

$$TIE = \frac{EBIT}{Int} \qquad (2)$$

where

$EBIT$ = Earnings before interest and taxes
Int = Interest expense

The times-interest-earned ratio is a multiple of the number of times that a firm's operating income requires operating interest payments. Clearly, a TIE of less than 1 is unacceptable. This would suggest that operating income is insufficient to make required interest payments. The higher the multiple, the higher the firm's debt capacity. This ratio should be compared to comparable firms or the industry.

The fixed-charge-coverage ratio measures the firm's ability to meet both interest payments and principal repayments.

$$FCC = \frac{(EBIT + LO)}{\left(LO + Int + \dfrac{SFP}{(1-t)} \right)} \qquad (3)$$

where

LO = Lease obligations

SFP = Sinking fund payments
  t = Marginal tax rate

The fixed-charge-coverage ratio measures in the numerator the amount of operating income ($EBIT$) before deducting any lease obligations that appear in $EBIT$ as fixed costs. Lease obligations are added back to this figure to remove the effect of a lease obligation deduction reported in EBIT. The denominator measures all fixed payments of the firm, including lease obligations, interest payments, and required debt repayments or sinking fund payments. Note that both lease obligations and interest payments are deductible; that is, they are paid from pretax dollars. On the other hand, sinking fund payments, or debt principal repayments, are paid from aftertax dollars and are not deductible. As a result, all sinking fund payments are grossed up to arrive at their equivalent pretax amount.[1] This ratio measures the ability of the firm to pay not only interest but also principal for a debt issue. Again, a ratio of less than one indicates that the firm does not have sufficient debt capacity to support an additional debt issue. The higher the ratio, the safer is the debt issue.

Along with other pro forma financial information, these ratios measure the current debt of the firm and any proposed additional debt. These ratios help form the basis for determination of debt capacity. However, they do not represent the entire process for determining the feasibility of a debt issue as compared to an equity issue. Additional considerations should include a sensitivity analysis of cash flows under various assumptions concerning economic conditions, sales level, interest rate changes, and competitive factors. These ratios and pro forma income statements and balance sheets are appropriate in each scenario.

Whenever a debt issue is not advised, an equity issue should be considered. An equity issue may be either a *straight equity* or an *equity-related* instrument. Straight equity is the issuance of common or preferred stock.

Common stock is an ownership stake in the firm with all residual rights of profits and losses. Because common stockholders absorb all risk—that is, do not receive a fixed or predetermined payment—the required rate of return is higher than for debt issues. This return to common shareholders is composed of dividend yield and anticipated capital gains.

$$K = \frac{D_1}{P_0} + g \qquad (4)$$

where

D_1 = Next period's dividend per share
P_0 = Current market price
g = Anticipated capital gain

A client anticipating the sale of common stock should closely analyze the anticipated return to new stockholders. The actual cost of issuing new stock must also be reflected so that the cost to the issuer will exceed expected return, as calculated in Equation (4).

Preferred stock returns to the shareholder a level dividend. This means that the growth factor in Equation (4) is not relevant for an issue of preferred stock. Often, preferred stock is cumulative, that is, it receives a current dividend and all dividends in arrears before any common stock dividend is paid. Because of this feature and the level dividend payment, preferred stockholders require a lower rate of return than do common stockholders. In a sense, preferred stock is a hybrid between bonds and common stock (it has a fixed dividend as with bonds, yet no maturity date as with common stock). Of course, the cost of flotation must be added to the expected return by preferred shareholders to arrive at an estimate of cost to the issuer.

An issuer may wish to avoid dilution of ownership and stock value associated with a common stock issue. A debt issue avoids the dilution of both control and stock value. However, if a debt issue is not well advised due to lack of debt capacity or debt servicing capability, a preferred stock issue can avoid an increase in the debt ratio while also maintaining common stock values and ownership percentages.

Another alternative for the issuing firm is an *equity-related security*. The most common equity-related instrument is a convertible bond. A convertible bond may be exchanged at a specified ratio for common stock of the same issuer. Preferred stock also may be issued in convertible form. For a less-seasoned issuer, a convertible instrument has certain advantages. With a convertible bond, the deduction for interest expense is maintained. Also, there is no dilution of ownership interest. With convertible preferred stock, dilution of ownership interest is avoided.[2]

There are also advantages for securities investors. Both bonds and preferred stock promise a fixed level of payment to the investor. Should the earnings stream of the issuing firm experience volatility or depressed results, the investor in a convertible instrument does not receive a diminished cash flow. On the other hand, if the earnings stream of the issuer is favorable and the value of the common stock increases, the owner of a convertible instrument may convert into common stock at the predetermined ratio. In other words, an investor in a convertible instrument has a floor built below expected cash flows but has no ceiling built above. Thus, upside potential may be realized while avoiding downside risk.

These considerations and others influence the decision to issue debt or equity. This decision should be driven by considerations specific to the issuer and environmental concerns with respect to investors and market conditions.

Floating versus Fixed-Rate Debt

Typically, debt issues are fixed-rate. The coupon rate describes the percentage of face value paid as interest per year during the life of the debt issue. Establishing the coupon rate for a debt issue is analogous to determining the appropriate expected return to shareholders for an equity issue. Establishing the coupon rate is similar to pricing a loan in a commercial banking context. As a commercial banker, a loan officer looks at the considerations with respect to the issuer's risk, the term of the loan, and market interest rates.

Essentially, an investment banker follows the same procedure. The difference is that often more public examples are available to help establish a coupon rate than a loan rate. One possible reference for determining a fixed rate is the yield for a comparable security or group of securities currently trading. If the debt issue will be rated by a credit rating agency, an estimate of appropriate yields can be determined by observing yields associated with securities of comparable rating. Another way of looking at the question of appropriate coupon rate is to estimate the appropriate spread over U.S. Treasuries of the same maturity.

The decision to issue a fixed-rate instrument depends on a number of factors. The issuer's balance sheet may suggest the need for long-term debt financing with a constant cost of funds. For example, a company with a number of long-term contracts at fixed contractual rates will be more interested in issuing long-term, fixed-rate debt. On the other hand, a firm whose revenues are highly correlated with the fluctuations in the overall economy will be less inclined to issue such instruments.

Another consideration when deciding to issue fixed-rate debt is the level of market interest rates. If market interest rates are likely to increase in the future, a long-term, fixed-rate debt issue is more desirable than a short-term or floating-rate alternative. The issuer prefers to lock in a relatively low cost of funds over the term of the debt issue. The problem with this strategy is that investors also have the same perception with respect to the direction of interest rates. A long-term, fixed-rate issue is less attractive to the investing public when they anticipate interest rates will increase. To sell the issue, the fixed-rate instruments must be associated with a higher rate of return or coupon rate than would otherwise be required.

The solution to such a problem is to associate a floating rate with the issue. Commercial bankers as loan officers are familiar with the process of establishing a floating-rate loan. Essentially, the interest rate is composed of two factors—an index or reference rate and a spread. The index rates for bank loans may be prime rate, the London Interbank Offered Rate (LIBOR), a cost of funds index, or Treasury rates. The spread is a constant percentage above the index rate. Thus, the variability of the floating-rate instrument is associated with the variability of the index rate.

The interest rate for public debt securities is commonly reset every three or six months. The index rate is typically LIBOR. In Eurobond issues, a floating-rate instrument is not uncommon. Particularly in the Eurobond market, several floating-rate instruments have developed.

- Perpetual floating-rate notes with no stated maturity.
- Capped floating-rate notes with an upper bound on the issuer's cost.
- Mini-max floating-rate notes that are variable only within a predetermined range.

Of course, participation in the Euromarkets requires that the issuer have a product line and/or reputation that will be appealing to international investors.

In advising clients as to the issuance of floating- or fixed-rate debt, investment bankers should remember that the issue is really a matter of which party assumes the interest rate risk. In a fixed-rate debt issue, the investors accept all the interest rate risk. In a floating-rate instrument, the issuer accepts all the risk. If a fixed-rate debt issue appears best from the perspective of the issuer, the investment banker must assist the client in determining the likelihood that investors will be prepared and willing to accept the associated interest rate risk.

Using Derivatives to Manage Interest Rate Risk

Deciding whether the issuer or the investor will assume the interest rate risk is a zero-sum gain. The nature of the stakes depend on the anticipated direction of interest rate changes and whether the instrument is fixed or floating rate.

- When interest rates are expected to increase, a fixed-rate instrument puts the investor at risk. The investor is locked into a lower interest rate than that which might prevail in the future. This is an *opportunity cost*. An opportunity cost is defined as cash flows that could have been received by investing in the next most attractive alternative, that is, cash flows that are forgone as a result of investing in the instrument in question. This opportunity cost is reflected in the market value of the security held by the investor. When interest rates increase, the market value of fixed-rate securities declines.
- When interest rates are expected to decrease, a fixed-rate instrument places the issuer at risk. Higher interest payments than would otherwise be required must be paid.
- When interest rates are expected to increase, a floating-rate instrument places the issuer at risk. As market interest rates increase, the cash flows required to service the debt also increase.
- When interest rates are expected to decline, floating interest rates place the investor at risk. As market interest rates decline, cash receipts by the investor also decline. This represents an opportunity cost for the investor because a fixed-rate instrument would not have resulted in decreased interest payments.

The risk associated with each of these four scenarios can be mitigated by the use of interest rate derivatives. Options on swaps, caps, and floors can protect the party at risk and perhaps reduce the overall cost of funding for the issuer. An investment banker should be prepared to discuss these alternatives and their associated costs.

Fixed-Rate Instruments and Anticipated Interest Rate Increases
In this situation, the fixed rate instrument investor is at risk that interest rates will increase, as shown in Exhibit 2–1. Should rates rise, the investor would have been better posi-

E X H I B I T 2–1

Trade-Off in Interest Rate Risk:
Issuer versus Investor

	Anticipated Direction of Interest Rate Changes	
	Increase	Decrease
Fixed-rate instrument	*Investor at risk:* Opportunity cost of not investing in an instrument whose rate of return will increase.	*Issuer at risk:* Higher interest cost than would otherwise be the case.
	Risk reduction: Investor buys a call option on a swap that entitles the investor to pay fixed rate and receive floating rate.	*Risk reduction:* Issuer buys a call option on a swap that entitles the issuer to receive fixed rate and pay floating rate.
Floating-rate instrument	*Issuer at risk:* Higher interest cost than would otherwise be the case.	*Investor at risk:* Opportunity cost of not investing in an instrument whose rate of return is fixed at a higher rate.
	Risk reduction: Issuer buys an interest-rate cap that entitles the issuer effectively to limit the amount of interest expense associated with the issue.	*Risk reduction:* Investor buys an interest rate floor that entitles the investor effectively to establish a minimum amount of interest income associated with the issue.

Source: Global Bank Research, 1995.

tioned with a floating-rate instrument. This exposure should
be hedged. The appropriate hedge maintains the relative
advantage of a fixed-rate instrument in a decreasing interest
rate environment from the perspective of the investor. An
option on a swap contract will accomplish this hedge.

An interest rate swap is an agreement to exchange
interest payments for a specified period. The interest pay-

ments are based on a *notional principal amount* that does not change hands. The most common swaps are coupon swaps exchanging fixed interest payments for floating interest payments. The swap market is dominated by commercial banks and governed by rules established by the International Swap Dealers Association, a self-regulatory organization.

Clearly, a swap can change a fixed rate instrument into the equivalent of a floating-rate instrument. However, an option on a swap or a *swaption,* may be a better alternative. A payor swaption would entitle the holder to pay a fixed rate on the notional amount and receive a floating rate. An American-style swaption would confer this right on any business day within the swaption period. Because this option entitles the holder to enter a swap agreement, it is referred to as a callable swaption; that is, a call option on a swap. If interest rates increase, the investor may exercise and effectively convert to a floating-rate instrument. Should interest rates remain stable or decrease, the investor would allow the swaption to expire unexercised.

Fixed-Rate Instruments and Anticipated Interest Rate Decreases

As also shown in Exhibit 2–1, in an anticipated environment of decreasing interest rates, the fixed-rate instrument may expose the issuer to higher interest costs than would otherwise be necessary. On the other hand, if interest rates increase, the issuer will be in a relatively favorable position. A swaption may also hedge this position. A receiver swaption entitles the owner to receive fixed-rate payments and obligates the owner to pay floating rates. The fixed-rate payments received by the issuer can satisfy its obligations under the terms of the fixed-rate issue. In this way, the cash outflows associated with the issue are offset by the cash inflows under the terms of the swap. The objective is for these two fixed-rate cash flows to net to zero. The issuer of the securities would then be obligated to pay floating rates under the terms of the swap. In other words, the issue would be converted to a floating-rate instrument. Should

interest rates decline after issuance of the fixed-rate security, the issuer would exercise the swaption and enter the
swap agreement. On the other hand, if interest rates
increase, the issuer should allow the swaption to expire
unexercised.

Floating-Rate Instruments and Anticipated Interest Rate Increases

When interest rates are expected to increase, a floating-
rate issue places the issuer at risk (see Exhibit 2–1). Higher
rates increase the cost of servicing debt. Of course, lower
rates decrease that cost. Thus, the unfavorable scenario
should be hedged. This is perhaps best accomplished when
the issuer buys a *cap*. Commercial bankers have used interest rate caps with both commercial loans and residential
mortgages.

With a securities issue, the principle is exactly the
same. A cap places a ceiling over the extent to which the
interest rate associated with the debt instrument may
increase. In the case of a cap, a notional principal is established as the basis for the transaction. While this term also
is used in the swap market, the cap is more similar to an
option in function. The *strike rate* is analogous to the strike
price of an option. The payment stream also is similar to an
option in that no cash flows are generated under the cap
agreement when interest rates remain below the strike
rate. On the other hand, the option is exercised automatically if interest rates rise above the strike rate. The price
paid for a cap is the *premium*. If the strike rate is set at the
current level of market rates, the premium may be relatively high. As the strike rate rises above the current
market rate, the premium declines. When the strike rate
reaches a level sufficiently above the current market rate,
the premium stabilizes.

Bankers in commercial or mortgage lending compare
the strike rate to the floating rate of the loan to determine
whether it will be activated or automatically exercised.
When a cap is purchased in the financial markets, the
strike rate is compared to an *underlying interest rate index*

that is a proxy for the level of general market interest rates. Often, the index rate is LIBOR but other rates may be used, such as the prime rate or the commercial paper rate. Under the terms of the cap, if the index rate is below the strike rate, no payments are forthcoming. On the other hand, if the index rate is higher than the strike rate, the owner of the cap is paid the differential interest rate applied to the notional principal for the appropriate period of time. The appropriate period of time is referred to as the *settlement frequency,* the number of times per year that cash flows may be exchanged. The objective is to select an index rate highly correlated to the floating rate of the debt security that is being hedged.

A number of factors determine the premium for a cap:

- *The strike rate.* A strike rate near current market rates tends to increase the premium while a higher strike rate tends to lower the premium.
- *Settlement frequency.* The more frequent settlement occurs, the higher is the premium.
- *Term of the contract.* A longer-term contract increases the premium.
- *Volatility of the index.* An index rate that is highly volatile increases the probability that the strike rate will be reached. A highly volatile index will increase the premium.
- *The shape of the yield curve.* A flat or inverted yield curve suggests future interest rates that are stable or declining. An upward sloping yield curve suggests higher interest rates in the future. An upward sloping yield curve, then, suggests a higher probability of the market rate reaching the strike rate and increases the premium.

Floating-Rate Instruments and Anticipated Interest Rate Decreases

As also noted in Exhibit 2–1, if interest rates are expected to decline, the investor is at risk of earning substantially lower than anticipated interest revenue. An

interest rate floor is the mirror image of an interest rate
cap. Instead of paying the owner in the event that the
index rate exceeds the strike rate, a floor pays in the
event that the index rate is lower than the strike rate. An
investor who buys a floor in connection with a floating-
rate instrument benefits if interest rates increase and is
protected should interest rates decline. Payments are
made to the owner of a floor based on the excess of the
strike rate over the index rate applied to the notional
principal for the appropriate period. Lowering the strike
rate tends to decrease the premium.

Pricing Considerations

An investment banker should discuss pricing alternatives
with its client to determine whether a derivative would
enhance the marketability of the issue and/or lower the
cost of funding. The pricing of these instruments is interre-
lated in that a swaption is a one-time option while a cap is a
series of options. The swaption must be exercised or it
expires with no impact on the transaction. Once a swaption
is exercised, however, the owner of the swaption is committed to the swap arrangement until the term of the arrangement has elapsed or until the arrangement is terminated.
On the other hand, a cap or floor is a series of short-term
options for the periods implied by the settlement frequency.
The interest-rate cap or floor confers protection to the
owner throughout the life of the contract. Once a swaption
has been exercised, the owner of the swaption is committed
to the obligations under the swap and has no further interest rate protection.

   An investment banker should discuss these issues, or
be prepared to discuss these issues, in terms of the particular situation associated with each client's debt issue. These
hedging techniques become increasingly important as the
role of securities markets expands. Because both issuers
and investors are better educated about the impact of
interest rate volatility, the all-or-nothing shift of interest
rate risk to one or the other increasingly becomes unacceptable.

Public versus Private Placement

A *public offering* of securities is intended for sale to the general public, whereas a *private placement* is sold to a small group of investors. Any public offering of securities in the United States offered to American investors is required to be registered with the Securities and Exchange Commission (SEC). In addition, public issues must comply with *blue-sky laws* in the state of issue and sale.

SEC requirements are the primary challenge in a public offering. When a firm that has already issued public securities enters the primary market, that offering is referred to as a *public offering*. On the other hand, if the firm has never issued securities to the public at large, the offering is referred to as an *initial public offering*. The SEC places stringent disclosure requirements on the issuer in both a public offering and initial public offering. The agency's objective is to ensure that all potential investors have adequate information to make informed decisions. The only exceptions to this general rule are securities with an initial maturity of 270 days or less (commercial paper) or securities offered for private placement.

Because private placements bypass the process of SEC registration, they are faster and more flexible. The ability to offer a private placement is based on the Securities Act of 1933. In this legislation, the formal requirements for SEC registration were established. This same legislation made clear that investors who could be considered knowledgeable and sophisticated need not be protected. The responsibility for obtaining adequate information prior to investment is shifted to investors in a private placement. In fact, the terms of a private placement are negotiated between the issuer and the investor. This is unlike the public offering in which the deal is structured and offered to the public after these decisions have been made.

While an unlimited number of potential investors that may be approached to purchase a private placement (since the 1982 issuance of Regulation D), the SEC does require that these investors be able to demonstrate both the capacity and intent to hold the securities for an extended period. The investors that can make such commitments and demonstrate such capacity and intent are large financial institutions (insurance companies, private pension funds, and public pension funds).

Commercial banks have been especially active in private placements because there is no need to take title to the securities before they are sold to the ultimate investor. Activities by commercial banks in private placements demonstrate the transferability of skills gained in the commercial lending/underwriting arena to an expanded role in investment banking.

For the issuer, the advantage of a private placement is that the costs associated with a public offering may be reduced or avoided; these include flotation costs (underwriting spread and out-of-pocket expenses) and administrative costs of managing the issue. Also, issuers may place their securities more quickly than is possible with a public placement. In addition, deals can be customized to meet the needs of both the issuer and the investor without concerns for features that would make the securities more acceptable to a wider investor pool. Private placements also may be advisable if the firm has a limited credit history, that is, if it is unrated or has a credit rating that is less than investment grade.

The typical structure of a private placement involves 35 or fewer investors, all of whom sign an *investment letter*. The investment letter states that securities will not be resold for a specific period, usually two years. However, the issue may be associated with a provision that permits later registration with the SEC to improve its marketability. In addition, Rule 144A premits privately held securities to be resold to institutional investors without registration with the SEC. The investment banker's role is to identify investors and to actively participate in the process of negotiating terms of the issue.

THE PUBLIC OFFERING

The success of a public offering of securities depends on the ability of the investment banker to analyze the client, potential investors, and market conditions. In addition, the

investment banker has obligations to other investment
banking firms participating in the transaction.

The Lead Manager

The investment bank that wins the mandate to run an issue
of new securities for a client is referred to as the *lead manager* or *bookrunner*. The lead manager's responsibility is to
ensure that the issuing firm complies with the disclosure
requirements of the SEC. These disclosure requirements
include an investigation into the issuer of the securities and
the structure of the deal. The 1933 Securities Act refers to
this as a *due diligence* investigation. The law requires that
the lead manager perform "a reasonable investigation" of
the issuer. Failure to do so results in the lead manager
being held responsible for the consequences of such failure.

The results of the due diligence investigation are contained in the issuer's *prospectus*. This legal document states
the purpose of the security issue, including details with
respect to the primary business of the issuer, the issuer's
financial condition, and principal officers. The prospectus
also describes the method of offering the securities for sale
and any interest or dividends to be paid. Essentially, the
prospectus is the method by which the lead manager and
other participating investment bankers offer the securities
to the public. The lead manager must ensure that all steps
necessary to reach the stage of public offer are taken.

The position of the lead manager in the transaction
may cause a tension between the issuer and the lead manager. The investment banker that wins the mandate must
have some confidence in the viability of the new issue. However, this enthusiasm may not be excessive. On the other
hand, the issuing firm may have a tendency to adopt the
most optimistic view of the prospects of the issue and of the
firm. As a result, management of the firm may view the
prospectus as a promotional vehicle. The lead manager
must resist the temptation to promise too much. In fact, the
lead manager may prefer to de-emphasize optimistic future
assessments of the firm to avoid later charges of misrepre-

sentation. This is clearly a delicate balance. The lead manager also makes sure that all of the securities are sold. The correct balance is to include all information that could possibly have an impact on the decision-making process of investors. The objective facts of the firm, its market position, financial results, quality of management, and product innovations should be included to enable potential investors to assess the viability of the issue.

The prospectus must be approved by the SEC. To begin the registration process, the lead manager prepares the preliminary prospectus, often referred to as the *red herring*.[3] The second portion of the preliminary filing contains any appropriate supporting documentation, including legal documents and financial data. In addition, a draft of the underwriting agreement is included. These documents are made available to the public at SEC offices. Within 20 business days of the filing of the red herring, the SEC comments on the preliminary filings. Based on these comments, the lead manager modifies the prospectus and addresses concerns of the SEC. The revised registration statement is submitted to the SEC. If there are no further comments, this becomes the final registration statement.

Note that this process has been significantly streamlined since 1982 with *Rule 415*. This rule was an attempt, on an experimental basis, to streamline the registration process under the SEC. The objective was to reduce the cost of issuances in the United States and to speed the offering process. This *shelf registration* permits issuers to register securities that they expect to sell within two years of the initial effective date of approval, eliminating the need to file additional registration statements with each subsequent offering. For issuers, the advantage is that they may move quickly to issue securities when market conditions appear most favorable. This arrangement requires issuers to report to the SEC any changes in financial conditions during the two-year period. Under shelf registration, securities may be issued with as little as 24 hours' notice to the SEC.

Shelf registration was so well received that the year after its introduction the experiment became a rule for all.

Since then, the SEC has approved the use of shelf registrations by limited partnership tax shelters, employee benefit plans, and issuers of mortgage pass-through certificates. SEC fees must be paid for all securities anticipated to be issued for the two-year period, however. To avoid paying excessive fees at the time of the Rule 415 filing, firms may file for only those securities to be issued in the near term and then subsequently modify the filing when additional securities are to be issued.

While the registration process is occurring, five other steps in the process are taking place:

1. The red herring is being printed in sufficient quantities to distribute to the public.
2. The appropriate filings under blue-sky laws in those states in which the securities will be sold are initiated.
3. Stock or bond certificates are printed.
4. The lead manager forms the underwriting syndicate.
5. The lead manager and members of the underwriting syndicate promote the issue in a *road show*.

During a road show, investment bankers and the issuing firms' management travel to various cities to speak to the investing public. Their pesentations explain the company and its management. Both bankers and managers make themselves available to answer questions that arise.

While it is the primary responsibility of the lead manager to conduct the due diligence investigation and to coordinate the SEC filings, the syndicate shares the responsibility for purchasing and distributing the securities to be issued.

The Syndicate

The *syndicate* is a term applicable to the functions of underwriting and distribution. The *underwriting syndicate* is the group of investment bankers that take responsibility for selling the securities. The *distribution syndicate* consists of the underwriting syndicate and a selling group. The selling group bears no underwriting risk.

Underwriting Syndicate

The underwriting syndicate reaches an agreement with the issuer that the securities will be sold under a firm commitment, a best efforts, or a standby underwriting. The issuer and the syndicate must agree on the pricing of the securities, the quantity to be sold, and the proceeds to the issuer. Because they receive the difference between the price charged to the investing public and the price promised to the issuer, the underwriters have a natural tendency to reduce the price paid to the issuer. On the other hand, the issuer has a natural tendency to maximize the price received. If this natural tension is not resolved, a firm commitment is unlikely. The issue may instead become a best efforts underwriting.

Note that initial public offerings (IPOs) are difficult to price. There is no seasoned security to which these new securities may be compared. Underwriters resist pricing that is overly optimistic because the underwriting syndicate bears the ultimate risk and the degree of market uncertainty is large. As a result, IPOs often are associated with significant price increases after the initial underwriting.

To at least partially counterbalance this phenomenon, the National Association of Securities Dealers (NASD) established rules that prohibit underwriters from selling the securities for more than the price indicated in the prospectus during the underwriting period. Whenever the securities are priced at substantially less than the price at which the market is willing to purchase them, the syndicate cannot increase the price and reap a windfall profit. Of course, if the market is softer than originally anticipated—that is, the market is willing to pay substantially less than the price indicated in the prospectus—the underwriting syndicate must absorb the loss.

While the issue is being approved by the SEC, negotiations as to price and terms continue. Once final SEC approval has been received, the issuer and the syndicate engage in final negotiations of all underwriting terms. The date on which this occurs is referred to as the *offering date*. The final terms include:

- Price of the offering.
- Size of the offering.
- Gross underwriting spread.

This information is provided to the SEC in an amendment to the prospectus. The following day a *tombstone* is published in the financial press. The tombstone advises the public that an offering of securities is being made. However, the securities are not formally offered through this tombstone advertisement. The prospectus is the only basis on which sales of the securities may be made.

Distribution Syndicate

The distribution syndicate is composed of the underwriting syndicate and a selling group. The participants of the underwriting syndicate include:

- Managers.
- Bulge bracket.
- Major bracket.
- Mezzanine bracket.
- Submajor bracket.

The lead manager is a member of the group of managers. The lead manager is designated by the issuer and, with a consent of the issuer, forms the syndicate. Syndicate members should be selected so they represent a strong portfolio of all capabilities required for successful underwriting. The managers' names appear initially in a tombstone, with the lead manager generally listed first. Next on the tombstone are the bulge bracket firms. The bulge bracket consists of the largest investment banking firms in the country. The term is derived from the appearance of their names when placed in tombstone advertisements—typically large and boldface.[4] The managers and the bulge bracket constitute the first tier of investment bankers. The second tier of investment bankers is referred to as the major bracket, while the third tier is referred to as submajors. The mezzanine bracket consists of small firms that have special relationships with either the issuer or the lead manager.

These firms are then divided into groups for the distribution of the securities. The breakdown of the distribution syndicate is

- Managers.
- Preferred group of dealers.
- Nonpreferred dealers, or selling group.

The managers are responsible for selling the bulk of the securities. The preferred group of dealers includes the managers and other members of the underwriting syndicate. Thus, the nonpreferred dealers, or selling group accept no underwriting risk under a firm commitment arrangement.

The lead manager helps to stabilize the price of the security during the underwriting period by agreeing to purchase the securities at the offer price. This assures investors of sufficient liquidity in the market. Often, the lead underwriter continues to make a market in the securities after the underwriting period. The commitment of the lead manager to purchase securities at the offer price is a *stabilizing bid*.

Compensation
The varying amount of risk accepted by the members of the distribution syndicate is reflected in the compensation arrangements of a securities issue.

- The *management fee* is compensation to the managers for their participation in preparing the securities offering. Accepting the responsibility for a thorough and diligent investigation is the primary basis for this compensation. Twenty percent of the gross underwriting spread (the difference between the offering price and the price paid to the issuer) typically is allocated for this purpose.
- The *underwriting fee* is also typically 20 percent of the gross underwriting spread. This portion of the

compensation covers expenses such as advertising, legal expenses, stabilization expenses, postage, and other related out-of-pocket expenses. Not covered by the underwriting fee are those expenses that are the responsibility of the issuer, including fees for SEC filings, issuer-related legal fees, accounting fees, and printing fees. Any excess of the underwriting fees over the 20 percent allocation is covered by syndicate members based on their participation in the issue. Should the 20 percent allocation exceed actual underwriting fees, the excess is allocated among participants in the same way.

- The selling concession is normally 60 percent of the underwriting spread. This compensation is allocated among the participants based on the securities they accept to sell. Selling representatives within the firms of the syndicates receive a portion of the selling concession. Should the syndicate members use nonpreferred dealers or selling group members for a portion of their securities allocation, the selling group participant may receive as much as half of the selling concession that applies.

THE SUCCESSFUL UNDERWRITING

Successful securities underwriters have both (1) a strong perception of their clients' capabilities and financial position and (2) a keen awareness of market conditions. The ability to work within a syndicate environment requires good timing and good relationships. It is also necessary to have an appreciation for the likelihood of changes in the general economy, especially with respect to interest rates and economic expansion or recession. Perhaps the most successful underwriting teams formed within a commercial bank consist of the commercial lending officers and securities trading officers. An underwriting team composed of both these competencies may be best prepared to both analyze and market an issue of new securities.

SELECTED REFERENCES

Das, Satyajit. *Swap & Derivative Financing: The Global Reference to Products, Pricing, Applications and Markets.* rev. ed. Chicago: Probus Publishing Company, 1994.

Fitch, Thomas. *Dictionary of Banking Terms.* Hauppauge, NY: Barron's Educational Series, 1990.

Howe, Donna M. *A Guide to Managing Interest-Rate Risk.* New York: New York Institute of Finance, 1992.

Marshall, John F., and M. E. Ellis. *Investment Banking and Brokerage: The New Rules of the Game.* Chicago: Probus Publishing Company, 1994.

ENDNOTES

1. The process of grossing up sinking fund payments is equivalent to finding the taxable equivalent amount related to municipal bond interest payments. Both of these calculations are based on the logic that after-tax cash flows are equal to before-tax cash flows, less taxes. The logic is as follows:

$$AT = BT - \text{tax}$$
$$= BT - BT\,(t)$$
$$= BT\,(1-t)$$
$$\therefore BT = \frac{AT}{(1-t)}$$

2. Preferred stock dividends are not deductible, as is true for common stock dividends.

3. This document is referred to as a red herring because its cover contains a statement in red lettering alerting prospective buyers that SEC approval is not final.

4. Bulge bracket firms are responsible for the largest number of underwritings and dollar amount of securities issued. Even though rankings vary by year and by classification of securities, common names in this category are Merrill Lynch, Goldman Sachs, Morgan Stanley, Salomon Brothers, and CS First Boston.

CHAPTER 3

Underwriting of Treasury and Municipal Bonds

INTRODUCTION

Commercial banks have participated in the primary securities market for Treasury securities and certain municipal bonds without interruption. The Glass-Steagall Act did not prohibit this activity when it called for the separation of commercial and investment banking. The act was aimed primarily at corporate securities activity and the perceived conflicts of interest associated with these activities. As a result, commercial banks and investment banks are direct competitors in these markets.

Because both markets are debt markets, commercial bankers that enter the investment banking arena with a strong commercial lending background may transfer these skills to the public market for Treasury and municipal debt. Treasury securities are free of default risk and offered in periodic auctions. The default risk of municipal bonds varies widely and securities are issued in a process similar to a corporate underwriting. Increasingly, municipal bonds are insured by third parties to increase their marketability.

UNDERWRITING POWERS OF COMMERCIAL BANKS

The federal law that grants commercial banks the power to underwrite Treasury and municipal bonds is Title LXII of the Revised Statutes of the United States, Chapter 1, Section 5136. In this section, national banks are permitted to conduct the normal business transactions of a corporation. In addition, national banks are given the power to conduct banking business. Among those powers specified are discounting and negotiating promissory notes, drafts, bills of exchange, and other evidences of debt; receiving deposits; buying and selling foreign exchange, coin, and bullion; and lending money on personal property. The Banking Act of 1933 amended this law to preclude national banks from being involved in securities activities.

> The business of dealing in securities and stock by the association shall be limited to purchasing and selling such securities and stock without recourse, solely upon the order, and for the account of, customers, and in no case for its own account, and the association shall not underwrite any issue of securities or stock.[1]

At the same time, provision was made for ownership of securities and limited underwriting powers. To the extent that the comptroller of the currency permits, national banks may hold investment securities for their own accounts. According to Title LXII, investment securities are "marketable obligations evidencing indebtedness of any person, copartnership, association, or corporation in the form of bonds, notes and/or debentures commonly known as investment securities under such further definition of the term investment securities as may by regulation be prescribed by the Comptroller of the Currency." The ownership of these debt securities was limited by the law to no more than 10 percent of capital stock and unimpaired surplus. However, the law did not authorize "the purchase by the association for its own account of any shares of stock of any corporation."

The law goes on to list a number of underwriting activities that may be conducted by national banks. This list of exceptions has grown over time, but includes only debt securities of the U.S. Treasury, government agencies, political subdivisions, and multinational organizations.

A national bank may deal in, underwrite, and purchase for its own account investment securities that fall into one of the following categories described.

- Obligations of the United States.
- General obligations of any state or of any political subdivision thereof.
- Obligations of the Washington Metropolitan Area Transit Authority that are guaranteed by the Secretary of Transportation under Section 9 of the National Capital Transportation Act of 1969.
- Obligations issued under authority of the Federal Farm Loan Act, as amended, or issued by the 13 banks for cooperatives or any of them or the Federal Home Loan Banks.
- Obligations insured by the Secretary of Housing and Urban Development under Title XI of the National Housing Act.
- Obligations insured by the Secretary of Housing and Urban Development (Secretary) pursuant to Section 207 of the National Housing Act, if the debentures to be issued in payment of such insured obligations are guaranteed as to principal and interest by the United States.
- Obligations, participations, and other instruments of or issued by the Federal National Mortgage Association or the Government National Mortgage Association; or mortgages, obligations, or other securities that are or have ever been sold by the Federal Home Loan Mortgage Corporation; pursuant to Section 305 or 306 of the Federal Home Loan Corporation Act.
- Obligations of the Federal Financing Bank.
- Obligations of the Environmental Financing Authority.

- Obligations or other instruments or securities of the Student Loan Marketing Association.

- Such obligations of any local public agency (as defined in Section 110(h) of the Housing Act of 1949) as are secured by an agreement between the local public agency and the Secretary, in which the local public agency agrees to borrow from said Secretary and said Secretary agrees to lend to said local public agency, monies in an aggregate amount which (together with any other monies irrevocably committed to the payment of interest on such obligations) will suffice to pay, when due, the interest on and all installments (including the final installment) of the principal of such obligations, which monies under the terms of said agreement are required to be used for such payments.

- Obligations of a public housing agency (as defined in the United States Housing Act of 1937, as amended) as are secured (1) by an agreement between the public housing agency and the Secretary, (2) by a pledge of annual contributions under an annual contributions contract between such public housing authority and the Secretary if such a contract shall contain the covenant by the Secretary that is authorized by subsection (b) of Section 22 of the United States Housing Act of 1937, as amended, or (3) by a pledge of both annual contributions under an annual contributions contract containing the covenant by the Secretary that is authorized by Section 6(g) of the United States Housing Act of 1937 and a loan under an agreement between the local public housing agency and the Secretary. In either of the three cases, these arrangements (together with any other monies committed to the payment of interest on such obligations) must be sufficient to cover the required payments of interest and principal.

- Obligations issued by the International Bank for Reconstruction and Development, the European

Bank for Reconstruction and Development, the Inter-American Development Bank, the Asian Development Bank, the African Development Bank, the Inter-American Investment Corporation, or the International Finance Corporation.

- Obligations issued by any state or political subdivision or any agency of a state or political subdivision for housing, university, or dormitory purposes, which are at the time eligible for purchase by a national bank for its own account.

- Bonds, notes, and other obligations issued by the Tennessee Valley Authority or by the United States Postal Service.

- Qualified Canadian government obligations to the same extent that such association may deal in, underwrite, and purchase for such association's own account obligations of the United States or general obligations of any state or of any political subdivision thereof. Qualified Canadian government obligations are backed by Canada, any province of Canada, or any political subdivision of any such province to a degree comparable to the liability of the United States, any state, or any political subdivision thereof for any obligation that is backed by the full faith and credit of the United States, such state, or such political subdivision. Qualified Canadian government obligations also include debit obligations of any agent of Canada or any province or any political subdivision when the obligation of the agent is assumed in its capacity as agent.

The preceding list of underwriting powers includes a wide variety of instruments. Additional powers have been granted to commercial banks under Section 20 of the Glass-Steagall Act by the Federal Reserve. Many of these activities overlap the two regulatory frameworks. For example, municipal general obligation bonds may be underwritten by national banks under the power just noted, while municipal revenue bonds may be underwritten only by permission of the Fed. In addition, government agencies issue mortgage-backed securities that are permitted by the act, while other asset-backed securities may be underwritten only under the authority of the Fed. Furthermore, the market for asset-backed securities, or securitized assets, is growing rapidly in the private sector. Accordingly, we discuss these topics in the context of the regulatory framework under which they are permitted.

- This chapter examines Treasury and municipal general obligation bonds.
- Chapter 4 examines powers conferred under a Section 20 subsidiary, including municipal revenue bonds and corporate securities.
- Chapter 5 discusses the entire range of asset-backed securities, including those issued by government agencies (permitted under the previously noted legislation) and those issued in the private sector (permitted only under special permission from the Federal Reserve).

TREASURY SECURITIES

Treasury securities are obligations of the U.S. government that are issued in three forms:

1. Treasury bills (T-bills)
2. Treasury notes (T-notes)
3. Treasury bonds (T-bonds)

All of these securities are issued in the primary market via an auction process. They are differentiated with respect to original maturity, method of interest payment, and day/count conventions.

Characteristics of Treasury Securities

Treasury securities may be distinguished by *original maturity*. T-bills have an original maturity of one year or less—three months (13 weeks or 91 days), six months (26 weeks or 182 days), and one year (52 weeks or 364 days). In addition, cash management bills are issued periodically to cover funding gaps. T-bills are issued on a discounted basis, that is, at an amount that is always less than face value with no interest payments between date of issue and date of maturity. The difference between purchase price and maturity value is interest income to the investor. This interest income is calculated on the basis of a 360-day year and the actual number of days between purchase and maturity.

$$P_0 = 100 - 100(k)\left(\frac{N}{360}\right) \tag{1}$$

where

P_0 = Current market price of T-bill
k = Rate of return/interest rate
N = Number of days before maturity

T-notes are issued with original maturities of 2, 3, 5, and 10 years. T-bonds have original maturities of between 10 years and 30 years, with 30-year bonds currently being issued. Both T-notes and T-bonds are coupon-paying instruments. The *coupon rate* is the percentage of face value of the bond that is paid per year in interest. T-notes and T-bonds pay interest on a semiannual basis. The actual interest payment received per six-month period is one-half the interest implied by the instrument's coupon rate. Thus, T-notes and T-bonds are priced as the present value of the annuity of interest payments plus the present value of the maturity value.

$$P_0 = Int \ (PVIFA_{k,n}) + M(PVIF_{k,n}) \tag{2}$$

where

Int = Periodic interest payment
= $\dfrac{(CR)(M)}{m}$
CR = Coupon rate
M = Maturity or face or par value

m = Number of interest payments per year
$PVIFA$ = Present value interest factor of annuity
$PVIF$ = Present value interest factor

(See the Appendix for $PVIFA_{k,n}$ and $PVIF_{k,n}$ values.)
Because T-notes and T-bonds pay interest based on a coupon rate, often they are referred to as *coupons* to differentiate them from discounted T-bills.

Prices for T-bills are quoted on the basis of yield, k. For T-notes and T-bonds, price is quoted as market value as a percentage of $100 of face value. The fractional portion of the price for T-notes and T-bonds is quoted in 32nds. As implied by Equation (1), the day/count convention for T-bills is actual days and a 360-day year. On the other hand, interest is accrued for T-notes and T-bonds on the basis of actual days and a 365-day period.

Because Treasury securities are issued frequently, it is not unusual to have both new issues and seasoned issues of the same remaining maturity.[2] A newly issued Treasury security of a given maturity is referred to as an *on-the-run* issue, while an older issue of maturity is referred to as an *off-the-run* issue. On-the-run issues are considered most liquid, and, as a result, trade at more narrow bid-asked spreads.[3] Investors and traders in the secondary market prefer the greater liquidity of the on-the-run issues and pay a premium for them.

The Primary Market for Treasuries

Treasury securities are issued in book-entry form, that is, there is no physical certificate. Ownership of Treasury securities is recorded electronically at banks, brokerage firms, government securities dealers, and the Federal Reserve. Regular auctions are conducted by the U.S. Department of the Treasury with the assistance of the Federal Reserve system, with the Federal Reserve Bank of New York playing a particularly pivotal role.

Exhibit 3–1 summarizes the frequency of auctions for T-bills, T-notes, and T-bonds. In addition, the maturity dates of the respective securities are indicated.

EXHIBIT 3–1

Treasury Auctions

Type of Security	Auction Frequency	Maturity Dates
BILLS		
13 week	Weekly	Each Thursday
26 week	Weekly	Each Thursday
52 week	Every fourth week	Every fourth Thursday
Cash management	As needed	Thursday
NOTES		
2 year	Monthly	Last calendar day of month
3 year	Quarterly	15th calendar day of February, May, August, November
5 year	Monthly	Last calendar day of month
10 year	Quarterly	15th day of February, May, August, November
BONDS		
30 year	Semiannually	15th day of February, August

Source: Federal Reserve Bank of New York, November 1995.

- The 13-week and 26-week T-bills are auctioned each week. The auction is announced on Tuesday with the actual auction occurring on the following Monday. The new T-bills are actually issued on the Thursday following the auction (settlement date). These instruments also mature on Thursdays.
- The 52-week bills are auctioned every fourth week. On each fourth Friday, the next 52-week auction is announced with the auction date occurring in the following month on the fourth Thursday. The settlement date is the Thursday following the auction. These T-bills mature every fourth Thursday. As 52-week T-bills approach maturity, they become fungible (easily exchanged or substituted) with 13-week and 26-week bills.

- Essentially, cash management bills follow the same auction schedule as 13-week and 26-week bills. However, they are issued only as cash management needs arise. They mature on Thursdays and are generally issued in early April, June, and December.
- Among the Treasury coupons, the two-year and five-year are on the same schedule. These are auctioned monthly on Tuesday and Wednesday, respectively. Auction dates occur during the week following announcement of the auctions. Announcements are on Wednesday of the week including the 20th of the month. Settlement date is the last calendar day of the month, as is the maturity date.
- The 3-year and 10-year notes are auctioned in what is referred to often as the quarterly refunding cycle. The 30-year Treasury bond was previously a part of this quarterly refunding, but now is issued on a semiannual basis. All of these Treasury securities mature on the 15th day of February, May, August, or November. Settlement dates correspond with these maturity dates. The quarterly refunding is announced on the first Wednesday of the mid-month of the quarter. The auction dates are Tuesday (3-year), Wednesday (10-year), and Thursday (30-year) of the week prior to the settlement date.

The Auction Process

Bids for Treasury securities may be submitted by government securities dealers (for clients or for their own accounts), individuals, or financial and nonfinancial corporations. On the date of an auction, bids are submitted to the Federal Reserve Bank in New York, or elsewhere, by 1:30 PM ET. Most of these bids are submitted by primary government securities dealers, but others may participate as well. Two types of bids are submitted:

1. *Competitive bids* include the amount of securities and yield. This yield is the minimum rate of return that the bidder wants to accept.

2. *Noncompetitive bids* include an amount only. Noncompetitive bidders understand that they will receive a yield based on the outcome of the competitive bidding process.

The Treasury accepts noncompetitive bids in the amount of $1 million or less for T-bills and $5 million or less for notes and bonds.[4] Historically, noncompetitive bids have constituted 10 to 25 percent of the total bids. These noncompetitive bids are accepted before competitive bids in the sense that the amount of available securities is reduced effectively by the amount of noncompetitive bids before competitive bids are considered. For example, an $11 billion auction with $4 billion in noncompetitive bids results in the allocation of only $7 billion to competitive bidders.

Competitive bids are accepted in ascending order of yield; that is, in descending order of price. The highest bid (lowest price) that is accepted is referred to as the *stop out bid*. When this yield is translated into a price, that price is referred to as the *stop out price*. The coupon rate or discount rate is then set based on the accepted competitive bids. The coupon rate or discount rate is set so that the average price paid for the securities is as close to par as possible. The actual price paid by the competitive bidders will be based on the yield of their bid and the issue's coupon or discount rate. Under this system, some of the competitive bidders pay a premium for the securities, others pay a discount, and still others pay close to par. Under this system the average competitive yield bid is close to the coupon rate of the issue. All noncompetitive bidders receive their securities at the average yield of competitive bids.

The Treasury has experimented with another approach to the auction process. In the so-called Dutch auction system, the yield to competitive bidders does not vary. While bids are submitted and accepted in ascending order of yield, the yield to winning competitive bidders is set at the highest-accepted competitive bid. At first glance, it appears that the Treasury may be paying a higher yield than would otherwise be the case. However, competitive bidders are motivated to enter a low enough yield bid to be included among the winners, while recognizing that they will be paid the highest yield among the winners. Essentially, the Dutch auction system means that all successful competitive bidders pay the stop out price. Because the coupon rate is determined in the same way as under the old system, the determination of coupon rate is not affected by this difference. Noncompetitive bidders receive their Treasuries at the same price as the competitive bidders.

By 3 PM ET of the auction day, the results of the auction are announced. The information that is released includes the stop out bid, parties that received allocations, the average yield accepted, and the lowest yield accepted. At auctions for a Treasury note or bond, the coupon rate is also announced. In addition, a measure describing the success of the auction is included. The *tail* is the difference between the stop out bid and the average bid. The tail is a measure of the difference between the highest bid (lowest price) and the average yield. If the tail is large, the auction is considered weak. On the other hand, if the tail is zero, the auction is considered very strong.

Foreign and international monetary authorities also participate in Treasury auctions. These parties are permitted to submit noncompetitive bids. However, instead of reducing the amount of securities offered during the auction, foreign noncompetitive bids add to the allocation. For example, if $11 billion in securities are to be auctioned, foreign noncompetitive bids result in more than $11 billion being issued. Assuming $4 billion in domestic noncompetitive bids and $2 billion in foreign noncompetitive bids, securities totaling $13 billion are issued:

- $7 billion to competitive bidders.
- $4 billion to domestic noncompetitive bidders.
- $2 billion to foreign noncompetitive bidders.

The additional securities offered through the auction are referred to as *add-ons*. For T-bills, add-ons occur only when the foreign bidder requests more new T-bills than those maturing in its portfolio. For example, if the foreign non-competitive bids noted in the preceding example were sub-mitted by an entity with $1 billion in maturing T-bills, add-ons would amount to only $1 billion. The remaining $1 billion (the maturing portion) would become a part of the competitive bidding process. If maturing T-bills amounted to $2 billion, there would be no add-ons—the entire $2 billion would be a part of the competitive bidding process. If the foreign bids were submitted by an entity with $3 billion in maturing T-bills, again, the $2 billion would be a part of the competitive bidding process.

Primary Government Securities Dealers

Primary government securities dealers are designated by the Federal Reserve Bank of New York (FRBNY). These firms are active in the primary and secondary market for Treasury securities. Exhibit 3–2 provides a list of the cur-rent primary government securities dealers. The group of 36 firms is roughly equally divided among commercial bank affiliates and securities firms. Also represented are foreign institutions, primarily commercial bank affiliates.[5]

New primary government securities dealers may either be commercial banks or broker-dealers. Banks are subject to official supervision by U.S. federal bank supervi-sors while broker-dealers must be registered with the Secu-rities and Exchange Commission (SEC) to qualify for status as a primary securities dealer. Certain capital standards must be met:

- Commercial banks must meet the minimum Tier 1 and Tier 2 capital standards under the Basle Capi-tal Accord. In addition, commercial banks must have at least $100 million of Tier 1 as defined in the Basle Capital Accord.
- Registered broker-dealers must have capital in excess of the SEC's or Treasury's regulatory warning levels and have at least $500 million in regulatory capital.

E X H I B I T   3–2

Primary Government Securities Dealers

BA Securities, Inc.
Barclays de Zoete Wedd Securities, Inc.
Bear, Stearns & Co., Inc.
BT Securities Corporation
Chase Securities, Inc.
Chemical Securities, Inc.
Citicorp Securities, Inc.
CS First Boston Corporation
Dean Witter Reynolds, Inc.
Deutsche Bank Securities Corporation
Dillon, Read & Co., Inc.
Donaldson, Lufkin & Jenrette Securities Corporation
Eastbridge Capital, Inc.
First Chicago Capital Markets, Inc.
Fuji Securities, Inc.
Goldman, Sachs & Co.
Greenwich Capital Markets, Inc.
HSBC Securities, Inc.
Aubrey G. Lanston & Co., Inc.
Lehman Brothers, Inc.
Merrill Lynch Government Securities, Inc.
J. P. Morgan Securities, Inc.
Morgan Stanley & Co., Inc.
NationsBanc Capital Markets, Inc.
Nesbitt Burns Securities, Inc.
The Nikko Securities Co. International, Inc.
Nomura Securities International, Inc.
Paine Webber, Inc.
Prudential Securities, Inc.
Saloman Brothers, Inc.
Sanwa Securities (USA) Co., L.P.
Smith Barney, Inc.
SBC Capital Markets, Inc.
UBS Securities, Inc.
Yamaichi International (America), Inc.
Zions First National Bank

Source: Market Reports Division, Federal Reserve Bank of New York, September 14, 1995.

- A bank or broker-dealer that wishes to become a primary government securities dealer must inform the FRBNY in writing.

The FRBNY consults with the appropriate regulatory entity to confirm that the firm is in compliance with these capital standards. Once accepted as a primary government securities dealer, the firm's capital position may not fall below these levels. If capital does fall below these levels, the trading relationship with the Fed may be suspended. In deciding whether such a suspension will be imposed, the FRBNY confers with the firm's federal regulator to determine whether the capital levels can reasonably be expected to be restored. Restoration of capital must be accomplished within a short time, however. The relationship may not be continued if stipulated minimum capital levels are not obtained within one year. Over time, this one-year grace period may be shortened and, in any event, would not apply if the firm's capital position were seriously impaired. Also, the FRBNY attempts to remain well informed about the creditworthiness of each primary government securities dealer.

Other conditions for a continuing trading relationship with the FRBNY as a primary government securities dealer are

- A primary government securities dealer must make reasonably good markets in the firm's trading relationships with the Fed's trading desk.
- In evaluating this aspect of the relationship, the FRBNY examines the amount of business of various types actually transacted. The Fed also evaluates the quality of the firm's market making. If a firm repeatedly submits bids that are not reasonably competitive, the firm may be dropped as a counterparty for at least six months.
- A primary government securities dealer must participate meaningfully in Treasury auctions. In evaluating this aspect of the relationship, the Fed expects a dealer to bid in reasonable relationship to

that dealer's scale of operation relative to the market and in reasonable price relationship to the range of bidding by other auction participants. In other words, a primary government securities dealer is expected to make a significant commitment of resources to the auction process and to enter bids that are well informed and reasonable in light of other market conditions. In deciding whether to suspend a dealer as a result of inadequate activity, the Fed confers with the Treasury Department.

• A primary government securities dealer is expected to provide the Fed's trading desk with market information and analysis that may be useful to the Federal Reserve in the formulation and implementation of monetary policy. Dealers are expected to bring to the Fed market information and commentary. If this aspect is not satisfied, the dealer is considered to contribute little to the efficient operations of the Fed and may be suspended for at least six weeks.

Also note that a foreign-owned primary government securities dealer may not be newly designated, or continue to be designated, if the Fed concludes that the country in which the foreign parent firm is domiciled does not provide the same opportunity for U.S. companies to underwrite and distribute government debt.

These requirements and guidelines make it clear that the dealers are selected for a number of reasons. Being able to provide feedback to the Fed is an important element of the designation. This necessarily means that a primary government securities dealer must make a commitment of resources for trading activity and for information management.

MUNICIPAL BONDS

Municipal bonds are issued by state governments, local governments, political subdivisions, and other entities such as school districts and agencies of state and local governments.

This is a growing market, with as many as 40,000 issuers. As the interest paid in connection with municipal bonds is tax exempt, these securities are popular among investors. Depending on the residence of the investor, interest income from municipals also may be exempt from state and local income tax. There are two general classifications of municipal bonds—general obligation bonds and revenue bonds.

General obligation bonds are issued by entities with taxing authority—cities, states, and other jurisdictions. They are secured by the taxing authority of the issuer. When the issuer has a limited purpose, such as a school district, the tax base also may be limited, perhaps a property tax authority. When the issuer has a wider range of taxing authorities, such as a city, all of these taxing sources collateralize the general obligation bonds. Accordingly, these bonds are sometimes referred to as *full faith and credit obligations*.

Revenue bonds are issued for specific purposes. They are repaid from the cash flows associated with that purpose. For example, a highway bond may be repaid from the proceeds of the toll assessed for users of the highway. Most revenue bonds are for public purposes, including bridges, tunnels, road systems, airports, colleges and universities, and utility projects. Some revenue bonds are issued for projects that can best be described as mixed public/private purposes. For example, a hospital that will be owned by private shareholders but provide needed care for indigent citizens is a private project with a public good.

The municipal bond market is both varied in terms of issuers and quite dynamic. At the same time, the market suffers from a lack of transparency and, sometimes, questionable market practices.

Municipal Bonds and the Tax Reform Act of 1986

Prior to 1983, commercial banks could earn tax-exempt income as well as deduct interest paid on deposits (and other funds) used to finance municipal bond investments. At the time, this practice was permitted only for depository institutions. Because of this tax preference, before the 1980s commercial banks invested in a large percentage of total municipal bonds outstanding. For example, in 1971, 51 percent of all municipal bonds were held in commercial bank portfolios. In 1983 Congress enacted legislation that partially restricted interest expense deductibility for commercial banks. After that year, only 80 percent of interest paid on liabilities used to finance municipal securities (tax-exempt securities) was deductible.

The net effect of this change is a kind of tax on tax-exempt securities. The Tax Reform Act of 1986 placed more restrictions on municipal bonds. These restrictions involved income exemptions and interest expense deductions. After 1986, only municipal bonds issued for public purposes retained complete tax exemption on interest income. Any municipal bonds issued for private purposes became subject either to alternative minimum tax or full taxation of interest income. In addition, commercial banks could no longer deduct interest expense on funds used to finance municipal bonds purchased after 1986. The only exception to this rule was public purpose bonds used by municipalities with $10 million or less in total issues per year. Because of these changes in tax law, qualifying municipal bonds are in great demand. Another result of the changes in the early 1990s was a drop in the share of total municipal bonds outstanding held by commercial banks to less than 15 percent.

A provision of the 1986 Tax Reform Act limited the flotation costs for private-purpose municipal bonds to 2 percent of the amount raised. This had the effect of dampening the interest of investment bankers for participation in the market. The effect of these changes is that the primary purchasers of municipal bonds today are individuals. This has resulted in the addition of features to municipal bonds that are attractive to individuals. Clearly, the exclusion of municipal bond interest from taxable income is an attraction. Increasingly, municipal bonds are being issued with insurance from third parties to back the bonds. The insurance phenomenon is partially in consideration of the number of consumers in the investor pool. It is also the result of the peculiarities of the market and its relative lack of transparency.

The Underwriting Process

Municipal securities are rarely sold directly to the investing public. Most often an underwriting syndicate brings the bonds to market.[6] In turn, the syndicate sells the municipal bonds to ultimate investors. Generally the underwriting agreement is negotiated. Some state laws require that underwriting engagements be subject to a competitive bidding process. Most revenue bond issuances are negotiated, while general obligation bond issues are roughly divided equally between negotiated underwritings and competitive bid underwritings.

When the underwriting is competitive, potential underwriters do not meet with the issuers to suggest structure or terms of the issue as is true in corporate securities issues. Instead, the issuer first publishes an official notice of the sale that includes the specifics including size of the issue, maturity, and conditions or restrictions that may apply. Examples of some distinctions relevant for municipal bonds include the issuance of serial bonds. Serial bonds are issues with maturity dates spread over a number of future periods. This creates several different tranches of the issue, one for each maturity date. At the same time, there may be a restriction that the tranches have coupon rates within a few basis points of each other. This can present a problem for investment bankers in that the restriction amounts to superimposing a flat yield curve on the issue. That is, an intermediate term bond may have the same yield as a long-term bond. When the yield curve is upward sloping (as it usually is), it may be necessary to sell some of the bonds at par while selling others above or below par. Such idiosyncracies cause municipal bond underwriting to be, in many ways, more challenging than corporate bond underwriting.

The underwriting process for municipal bonds follows very much the same functional process as that for corporate bonds—origination, underwriting, and distribution. However, there are some differences. The U.S. Constitution forbids the federal government to interfere with the fund-raising of states, and, by extension, local governments. This means that issuers are not required to register municipal bonds with the SEC. Effectively, municipal issuers are exempt from the registration requirements of the Securities Act of 1933.[7] The issuance of official statements by municipal securities underwriters has developed over time. The movement toward more due diligence on the part of municipal bond underwriters received considerable momentum during the 1970s when New York City experienced a bond crisis. In 1989, Rule 15c2–12 of the 1934 Securities Exchange Act was adopted, requiring that an underwriter of municipal securities deliver an official statement in connection with the primary issuance of municipal securities.[8] The 1989 ruling was prompted largely by the failure of Washington Public Power System bonds and the belief that insufficient information had been provided to investors prior to bond purchases.[9]

Underwriters' Disclosure Responsibilities

Because municipal securities are exempt from the Securities Act of 1933, disclosure requirements have been governed only by antifraud provisions that prohibit fraudulent or deceptive practices in the issuance of municipal bonds. Disclosures by municipal bond issuers must not contain false or misleading statements of material facts, including the omission of material facts whose omission would cause the statements to be misleading.

In the absence of federal regulation of disclosures, a number of voluntary guidelines have been established by associations involved in the municipal bond industry. Originally published in 1976 by the Government Finance Officers Association (GFOA, formerly the Municipal Finance Officers Association), the *Disclosure Guidelines for State and Local Government Securities* are composed of three sections—guidelines in connection with original offering of securities, ongoing disclosure, and procedures for distributing information to investors. The GFOA guidelines stress the voluntary nature of the suggestions and emphasize that adequate disclosure must always be from the viewpoint of the investor. These guidelines were revised in 1988 and 1991. A number of other sets of voluntary guidelines with comparable recommendations also have been published.

- *Disclosure Handbook for Municipal Securities*, National Federation of Municipal Analysts, 1992.
- *Recommendations for a Consistent Presentation of Basic Bond Provisions in Official Statements*, Public Securities Association, 1989.
- *Municipal Disclosure Task Force Report*, National Association of State Auditors, Comptrollers and Treasurers, 1990.
- *Codification of Governmental Accounting and Financial Reporting Standards*, 2nd ed., Governmental Accounting Standards Board, 1987.
- *Disclosure Format for Single-Family Mortgage Revenue Securities Issues*, National Council of State Housing Agencies, 1990.
- *Guidelines for Information Disclosure to the Secondary Market*, Association of Local Housing Finance Agencies, 1992.

After the failure of the Washington Public Power System bonds, the SEC adopted Rule 15c2–12. This rule requires that all municipal underwriters (banks and nonbanks) of primary market offerings of municipal bonds obtain and distribute to investors official statements from municipal issuers. Such official statements are required for all bond issuers whose principal amount is $1 million or more. As an agency of the federal government, the SEC may not interfere with the financing arrangements of state and local governments; this rule was adopted as a way of assisting underwritings in meeting responsibilities under the more generalized antifraud provisions of the Securities

Exchange Act of 1934. Under Rule 15c2–12, an underwriter must:

- Obtain and review an issuers' official statement that is "deemed final" by an issuer prior to making any bid for purchase, offer, or sale of municipal bonds.
- Deliver on request copies of the final official statement for a specified time. This period begins at the time the official statement is available until the earlier of (1) 90 days from the underwriting period or (2) the date when the official statement is made available to a nationally recognized municipal securities information repository. This period cannot be less than 25 days.
- Contract to receive within a specified period of time sufficient copies of the issuers final official report to comply with the delivery requirement.

Three specific types of municipal bonds offerings are exempted from these requirements. In each case, the offering of municipal bonds must be in denominations in $100,000 or more. In addition, any one of the three following conditions can exempt the issue from Rule 15c2–12:

1. No more than 35 investors, each of whom the underwriter reasonably believes is capable of evaluating the investment and is not purchasing the investment with the intent to distribute.
2. A maturity of nine months or less.
3. The ability to tender to an issuer (redeem), at the option of the investor, at least as frequently as every nine months.

Three firms have been designated as Nationally Recognized Municipal Securities Information Repositories (NRMSIRs): American Banker Bond Buyer, JJ Kenny Co., and Bloomberg L.P. Because supplying official statements to an NRMSIR reduces the length of time that a bond underwriter must supply the statements, many municipal bond underwriters have elected to make this information available to such repositories.

The content of the official statement by municipal bond issuers has been outlined by the Municipal Securities Rulemaking Board (MSRB). This self-regulatory organization was established by Congress in 1975 for brokers and dealers in municipal securities. The MSRB has 15 members from the municipal bond industry and from the public—5 members represent nonbank broker-dealers, 5 represent bank dealers, and 5 represent the public (associated with neither a broker, dealer, or municipal bond dealer). Of the five representatives for the public, one must represent municipal bond issuers. The MSRB has no inspection or enforcement powers. It is strictly a rule-making body for bank and nonbank municipal bond industry participants; any rules promulgated by the MSRB must be approved by the SEC. Most of the rules of the MSRB relate to secondary market activity and professionalism. Among others, these areas include professional qualifications, sales practices, recordkeeping, frequency of periodic compliance examinations, quotations, and advertising. The enforcement of MSRB rules is the responsibility of the SEC, the National Association of Securities Dealers (NASD), and bank regulators.

The SEC has broad disciplinary authority over all municipal securities, brokers, dealers, and associated dealers. Remedies available to the SEC include:

- Suspension, revocation, and denial of the registration of a broker or dealer or municipal securities dealer.
- Imposition of appropriate limitations on the activities of any person who violates the Securities Exchange Act and associated regulations.
- Initiation of independent administrative or judicial action against any municipal securities dealer that is a bank.

The NASD has the primary responsibility of overseeing the activities of nonbank municipal securities brokers and dealers. Its enforcement activities have focused on sales practice improprieties that involve excessive markups and inappropriate pricing. Remedies available to the NASD include:

- Censure.
- Imposition of a fine requiring restitution.
- Suspension of membership or suspension of registration.
- Expulsion from membership or revocation of registration.
- Imposition of any other "fitting sanction deemed appropriate under the circumstances."

Bank regulatory authorities include the Board of Governors of the Federal Reserve System, Federal Deposit Insurance Corporation, and the Department of Treasury—Comptroller of the Currency. These regulatory authorities are authorized to enforce compliance with MSRB rules by municipal securities dealers that are banks. In so doing, the bank regulatory authorities may use many of the same sanctions provided to the SEC. The Securities Exchange Act permits bank regulators to enforce MSRB and SEC municipal bond rules and regulations in accordance with the Federal Deposit Insurance Act. Included among the remedies for bank regulators are cease-and-desist orders that require an offending bank to cease-and-desist from any violation of municipal securities rules and regulations. For less severe infractions, a bank or its securities affiliate may negotiate and execute an agreement with the bank regulator outlining those steps needed to correct the violation. This disciplinary information is shared with the SEC and the MSRB via examination reports made available every six months.

The specific rule of the MSRB that relates to the initial issuance of municipal bonds and the official statement is Rule G–32. This rule requires that municipal securities brokers and dealers that sell securities to the public must deliver a copy of the final official statement or, if no final official statement is being prepared, a written notice to that effect. If the sale of the securities is negotiated with the underwriter, information must be disclosed in the final official statement with respect to the underwriting spread, amount of fees paid to the dealer, and the initial offering price for each maturity offered by the underwriters.

Because federal regulations may not interfere with the financing of states and local governments, these official statements have no standard format. As a result, there is wide variation in the content of the statements. Large municipal issuers typically provide thorough, highly detailed documents that meet or exceed the guidelines set by the GFOA. These statements typically include complete disclosure concerning the issuer, revenue sources, the use of funds to be raised, and the characteristics of the bonds to be issued. Smaller issuers that are less frequent partici-pants in a municipal bond market prepare less comprehen-sive statements. Some may include only a one- or two-page document geared primarily to assist in selling the issue.

Issues to Be Addressed as an Underwriter

Although the municipal bond industry is an attractive one for individual investors and has grown considerably in the last decade, any underwriting institution must be prepared to address a number of issues. Essentially, the municipal bond market is not as efficient as the market for Treasury securities and many corporate stocks. These issues are

- Ongoing disclosure.
- The appearance of impropriety.
- Pricing in the secondary market.

On-Going Disclosure

In addition to often inadequate disclosure on issuance of municipal bonds, the industry is faced with a lack of consis-tent ongoing disclosure. Even though municipal bonds are publicly traded, issuers are not required to prepare the equivalent of an 8-K or 10-K, as required by the SEC. Thus, the market operates with a general lack of public informa-tion throughout the life of the bonds. If an investment banker also intends to act as a market maker in the sec-ondary market, there are issues of disclosure related to bond trades. Many times, commissions are not disclosed on confirmations or brokerage statements. An investment banker intending to become an underwriter of municipal bonds must establish internal policies and procedures that avoid costly errors in connection with insufficient information about the financial position of the issuer, the reasonableness of the use of bond proceeds, the future prospects of the issuer's tax base or revenues, and material changes in any of these factors after issuance.

The Appearance of Impropriety

The municipal bond industry has as many as 50,000 issuers. This number is far greater than the issuers of corporate stocks and bonds. Furthermore, the extent of preparation in financial structuring that personnel employed by the issuer have received can be highly variable. The personnel of some issuers are well trained in the operation of financial markets and have considerable experience in the area. Other issuers have far less-experienced personnel.

When the municipal officers are less experienced, municipal bond underwriters may be exposed to subsequent criticism that they misled the personnel of the issuer by intentionally omitting important information or by misrepresenting material facts. For example, in the early 1990s, officials of the Pontiac, Michigan, school district sold $36 million in deferred-interest bonds. At the time, the bonds seemed a reasonable answer to the situation faced by the school district. These Capital Appreciation Bonds (CABs) functioned as zero-coupon bonds; interest was not paid in the early years of the issue but added to the principal. The issue enabled the school district to avoid a property tax increase in the early years and yet begin construction of needed educational facilities right away.

According to school district officials, they did not realize the magnitude of the obligation associated with the CABs until a few years later. School district officials now realize that they will end up paying $100 million in exchange for $36 million in bond sale proceeds. The school district brought legal action against its legal advisor and the securities firm that underwrote the issue, claiming that both were guilty of rendering poor advice and creating a conflict of interest in which the school district suffered.

Thus, one of the problems associated with the municipal bond industry is that investment bankers and underwriters can appear to be taking advantage of issuing states and municipalities. Becoming involved in municipal bonds means that an underwriter must take special precautions to advise the issuers of the consequences of the issue under various scenarios. An investment banker should communicate the impact of changing assumptions with respect to tax base, interest rate environment, general economic conditions, and any other relevant factor. Clearly, if derivative products are part of the financing arrangement, the underwriters must take special precautions to ensure that these derivative products are clearly understood in the context of an extensive scenario analysis.

Not only the investment bankers are subject to claims of impropriety in the municipal bond market. In some cases, issuers place conditions on winning a mandate unrelated to the quality or terms of the investment banking services. State and local politicians or city controllers may expect contributions to political campaigns in exchange for the mandate to underwrite the bonds. Any investment banker that is or intends to be involved in underwriting municipal bonds must carefully consider the firm's position with respect to this impropriety or appearance of impropriety.

The ethical issues in the municipal bond industry are clearly complicated by the lack of federal oversight that could establish a standard of behavior and a uniform response in the event of conflict of interest. Ultimately, the taxpayers of the issuing state or municipality and investors in the municipal bonds absorb the cost of these market inefficiencies. As a participant in the market, investment bankers must not only be aware of but also guard against the cost.

Pricing in the Secondary Market

Only a few of the most actively traded municipal bonds are quoted in the financial press. This is a mere fraction of the number of municipal bonds outstanding. Furthermore, few bonds rated lower than AA (the second highest rating) are included in these listings. For the vast majority of issues, an investor must contact a broker-dealer for a quotation on a municipal bond. To complicate matters, contacting two different dealers can result in two significantly different quotations.

The only objective source of pricing information is the *Blue List*. The Blue List is published by Standard & Poor's. The bonds listed represent municipal bond dealers' holdings available for sale. The price shown in the Blue List is the price at which the dealer would like to sell the bonds, not the actual prices at which bonds have sold. If an underwriter of municipal bonds elects to make a market in these bonds, market illiquidity and inefficient pricing must be considered. An investment banker that holds such securities in its own account is subject to the normal price volatility associated with changing interest rates and economic conditions. In addition, the value of any such bonds held by the investment banker is impacted by the peculiarities of this particular market.

Insured Municipal Bonds

The municipal bond market has shifted from being denominated by commercial bank investors to being denominated by individual investors. As noted earlier, in the early 1970s commercial banks held more than 50 percent of all municipal bonds. Today, individual investors hold approximately 75 percent of all municipal bonds outstanding. Given the variability in available information, the vast number of issuers, and the lack of a centralized market for secondary trading, it is perhaps not surprising that insurance coverage for the payment of principal and interest of municipal bonds is appealing and increasingly observed.

From the issuer's perspective, insurance substitutes the creditworthiness of the insurer for the creditworthiness of the issuer. Thus, an issuer with an A rating that obtains insurance coverage from a company with a AAA rating can receive a rating of AAA. This reduces the borrowing cost of the issuer and may more than offset the cost of the insurance coverage. By 1992, more than 34 percent of all new issues of municipal bonds were sold with bond insurance. Insurers of municipal bonds sell loan guarantees to issuers and, in the secondary market, sell guarantees to investors.

There are six full-service municipal bond insurers that currently provide coverage for the industry:

1. AMBAC Indemnity Corporation.
2. Capital Guaranty Insurance Corporation (CGIC).
3. Capital Markets Assurance Corporation (CapMAC).
4. Financial Guaranty Insurance Corporation (FGIC).
5. Financial Security Assurance, Inc. (FSA).
6. Municipal Bond Investors Assurance Corporation (MBIA).

These companies carry AAA ratings from Standard & Poor's Corporation and Aaa ratings from Moody's Investors Service.

From the perspective of bond insurers, municipal bond insurance is viewed differently than property and casualty insurance. In the latter case, the objective is to diversify risk over a large number of insureds while recognizing that there will be some claims. Bond insurance, however, is underwritten to the standard of zero-loss. In other words, a bond insurer attempts to satisfy itself that there will be no default. Becuase this guarantee is for the full term of the bonds, the underwriters of bond insurance attempt to take a long-term view of the issuer and the issue. Note these three points:

- The overall default rate is very low. According to data from the Bond Investors Association, less than 1.5 percent of the total number of long-term issues sold defaulted in the last decade.
- For those municipal bonds that are insured, bankruptcies are exceedingly rare. That is, even a default (such as a missed interest payment) is generally a passing phenomenon. Cities, towns, counties, school districts, and utilities generally work out any temporary debt problems.

- Bond insurance pays principal and interest when due. In most cases, there is no acceleration of the payment of interest and principal.

While the insurance premium clearly depends on the issuer and other circumstances, a 1 percent premium is a reasonable order of magnitude for the cost of protection. An investment banker that anticipates being involved in the municipal bond market must understand the importance of insurance and the rigorous evaluation associated with it.

VERY DIFFERENT MARKETS

The Banking Act of 1993 permitted commercial banks to act as underwriters for Treasury and municipal bonds. Although both activities are permitted, the two are vastly different. The Treasury market is very liquid with homogenous securities that are actively traded. Information about the issuer is known by all market participants. Conversely, the municipal bond market is characterized by myriad issuers for which information is highly variable. These very inefficiencies can cause the municipal bond market to be highly profitable. Clearly, the skills required to excel in the two markets are different. Nevertheless, both markets represent the possibility of increased revenues for commercial banks.

SELECTED REFERENCES

Jones, Frank J., and Frank J. Fabozzi. *The International Government Bond Markets*. Chicago: Probus Publishing Company, 1992.

Marshall, John F. *Investment Banking & Brokerage: The New Rules of the Game*. Chicago: Probus Publishing Company, 1994.

Thau, Annette. *The Bond Book: Everything Investors Need to Know About Treasuries, Municipals, GMNAs, Corporates, Zeros, Bond Funds, Money Market Funds, and More*. Chicago: Probus Publishing Company, 1994.

ENDNOTES

1. Title LXII of the Revised Statutes of the United States, Chapter 1, Section 5136, 7th paragraph.

2. A seasoned issue is one that has traded in the secondary market for at least one year and has an established track record.

3. Bid-asked spreads are the difference between the price at which a dealer purchases a security (bid) and the price at which a dealer sells that security (asked).

4. Noncompetitive bids also may be submitted directly to the Treasury Department in a system called Treasury Direct. Such bids must be submitted by noon on the day of the auction.

5. Note that Daiwa Securities America, Inc., was a primary government securities dealer until October 1995. At that time, it was disclosed that the firm had concealed information with respect to trading losses and a fraudulent cover-up of those losses from the Federal Reserve. In November 1995, Daiwa was indicted and lost its permission to operate in the United States.

6. See Chapter 2 for a discussion of the formation of the underwriting syndicate.

7. Note, however, that municipal issuers are subject to the antifraud provisions of the Securities Exchange Act of 1934.

8. In April 1975, New York City was unable to pay the interest on a short-term note and deferred the payment. Note that none of New York City's long-term bonds were ever involved in this problem. The interest was ultimately paid and no investor failed to receive the full amount of interest and

payments as originally contracted. Of course, anyone who sold the bonds realized a capital loss because the market value declined significantly. The resolution of the crisis involved the creation of the Municipal Assistance Corporation (MAC). This agency was empowered to issue bonds on behalf of New York City. MAC bonds were neither obligations of the city nor backed by the taxing authority of the city. Instead, the state of New York backed the bonds in exchange for a lien on sales taxes within the city and on a stock transfer tax. When the bonds came to market, they yielded 200 basis points above the yields on comparable bonds at the time, that is, 10 percent when comparable bonds were yielding 8 percent. The MAC bonds subsequently performed well with debt service coverage as high as 11 times. (See Chapter 2 for a discussion of debt coverage ratios.) In fact, the performance was so good that the credit rating of the bonds was increased from A to AA by 1990. Even though the New York City case was satisfactorily resolved, the episode raised concerns about the safety of municipal bonds and the adequacy of investor protection.

9. The Washington Public Power Supply System (WPPSS) was established by the state of Washington to produce and sell electric power to municipal and private power companies in the Northwest region of the country. WPPSS issued revenue bonds in 1977 to finance two new nuclear power plants, projects 4 and 5. The revenue bonds were supported by contracts to sell this power once the projects were completed. However, unforeseen cost overruns and lagging demand for power in the Northwest forced WPPSS to terminate construction of the plants in 1982. Bond holders were left holding worthless instruments. In a case tried up through the Washington State Supreme Court, judges ruled that government authorities had no legal grounds on which to pay principal and interest on the bonds from other revenue sources. This experience cost investors $2.25 billion and had a major impact on the revenue bond market. As a direct result, required yields on revenue bonds increased significantly, particularly those intended to finance wholesale power projects. The experience also had the effect of sharply escalating the concern for investor protection in the municipal bond industry.

CHAPTER 4

The Section 20
Subsidiary

INTRODUCTION

The Glass-Steagall Act, as part of the Banking Act of 1933, prohibits national banks from being involved in securities activities. Section 20 of the act prohibits national banks from affiliating with securities firms.[1] However, the Federal Reserve Board ruled in 1987 that bank affiliates could underwrite commercial paper, revenue bonds, and other securities. This ruling was challenged in federal court by the securities industry in *Securities Industry Association* v. *Board of Governors*. However, the position of the Federal Reserve was upheld by the U.S. Supreme Court in 1988. This permission was granted under Section 20 of the Glass-Steagall Act. Specifically, the act prohibits any member of the Federal Reserve from affiliating "with any corporation, association, business trust, or other similar organization engaged principally in the issue, flotation, underwriting, public sale, or distribution at wholesale or retail or through syndicate participation of stocks, bonds, debentures, notes or other securities."[2]

The Federal Reserve interpreted Section 20 to permit affiliating with a securities firm as long as that firm was not principally engaged in the prohibited securities activities. In 1989, revenues from underwriting the otherwise prohibited securities was capped at 10 percent of revenue of the securities affiliate. Because of this restriction, most banks with Section 20 subsidiaries have consolidated all of their securities activities (unrestricted and restricted) into one affiliate of their respective holding companies. The Federal Reserve is careful to ensure that there is a proper separation between the commercial banking business and the securities business within the holding company. One part of the approval process is an on-site examination of the physical premises. The Federal Reserve examiners audit to ensure (1) that Section 20 subsidiaries are not funded by deposits or bank holding company debt and (2) that fire-walls are in place to appropriately restrict transactions between the commercial bank affiliate and the Section 20 subsidiary.

Federal legislation is currently being considered to repeal Glass-Steagall. At this writing, the legislation has been passed by the U.S. Senate and will be reviewed by the U.S. House of Representatives. If this legislation passes, most bank holding companies will still be required to establish separate subsidiaries for securities activities. Thus, the function of a Section 20 subsidiary is a relevant model.

A securities affiliate expands the financial evaluation of clients to meet standards of feasibility and disclosure necessary in public securities markets. Some of the securities will be listed on organized exchanges such as the New York Stock Exchange or the American Stock Exchange. Other new corporate issues will be better suited to a NAS-DAQ listing in the computerized over-the-counter market. In addition, there are opportunities to underwrite a wide variety of municipal revenue bonds. The exact combination of underwriting capabilities depends on the location of the bank holding company and the strategic position of the firm in its market.

POWERS OF SECTION 20 SUBSIDIARIES

A Section 20 subsidiary may receive three levels of under-writing powers:

1. Municipal revenue bonds, mortgage-related securities, commercial paper, and consumer-receivable related securities.
2. Corporate debt.
3. Corporate debt and equity.

Authorized Subsidiaries

Exhibit 4–1 contains a list of the Section 20 subsidiaries as of June 30, 1995. Of these 37 institutions, 24 are U.S. banks and 13 are foreign banks. The foreign banks are concentrated in the New York, Chicago, and San Francisco districts of the Federal Reserve. Among the Section 20 subsidiaries are both money-center banks and large regionals. The number of Section 20 subsidiaries has increased over time. In 1990, there were 29 such affiliates. By 1993, the number had grown to 31. All of the organizations listed in Exhibit 4–1 have the first level of powers granted under Section 20 of the Glass-Steagall Act. In addition, the following institutions have corporate debt securities powers:

- First of America Bank Corporation.
- First Chicago Corporation.
- Barclays PLC Bank.

These institutions with Section 20 subsidiaries have equity powers as well as corporate debt powers:

- Banco Santander, S.A.
- The Bank of Nova Scotia
- Bankers Trust N.Y. Corporation
- Canadian Imperial Bank of Commerce
- Chase Manhattan Corporation
- Chemical Banking Corporation[3]
- CitiCorp

E X H I B I T   4–1

Section 20 Subsidiaries
(As of June 30, 1995)

Parent Organization	Section 20 Subsidiary	Date of Approval
Boston District		
Fleet Financial Group	Fleet Securities, Inc.	10/88
New York District		
Banco Santander, S.A.	Santander Investment Securities, Inc.	3/95
The Bank of Nova Scotia	ScotiaMcLeod (USA), Inc.	4/90
Bankers Trust N.Y. Corp.	BT Securities Corp.	4/87
Barclays Bank PLC	Barclays de Zoete Wedd Securities, Inc.	1/90
Canadian Imperial Bank of Commerce	Wood Gundy Corp.	1/90
Chase Manhattan Corp.	Chase Securities, Inc.	5/87
Chemical Banking Corp.	Chemical Securities, Inc.	5/87
Citicorp	Citicorp Securities, Inc.	4/87
Deutsche Bank AG	Deutsche Bank Securities Corp.	12/92
The Long-Term Credit Bank of Japan, Ltd.	Greenwich Capital Markets, Inc.	5/90
J. P. Morgan & Co.	J. P. Morgan Securities, Inc.	4/87
The Royal Bank of Canada	RBC Dominion Securities Corp.	1/90
Saban/Republic New York Corp.	Republic N.Y. Securities Corp.	1/94
Swiss Bank Corporation	SBC Government Securities, Inc.	12/94
The Toronto-Dominion Bank	Toronto Dominion Securities (USA), Inc.	5/90
Philadelphia District		
Dauphin Deposit Corp.	Hopper Soliday & Co., Inc.	6/91
Cleveland District		
Banc One Corp.	Banc One Capital Corp.	7/90
Huntington Bancshares, Inc.	Huntington Capital Corp.	12/92
Mellon Bank Corporation	Mellon Financial Markets, Inc.	4/95
National City Corporation	NatCity Investments, Inc.	2/94
PNC Bank Corp.	PNC Securities Corp.	7/87

EXHIBIT 4-1 (Concluded)

Parent Organization	Section 20 Subsidiary	Date of Approval
Richmond District		
First Union Corp.	First Union Capital Markets Corp.	8/89
NationsBank Corp.	NationsBanc Capital Markets, Inc.	5/89
Atlanta District		
Bank South Corp.	Bank South Securities Corp.	5/93
Barnett Banks Inc.	Barnett Securities, Inc.	1/89
SouthTrust Corp.	SouthTrust Securities, Inc.	7/89
SunTrust Banks, Inc.	SunTrust Capital Markets	8/94
Synovus Financial Corp.	Synovus Securities	9/91
Chicago District		
ABN AMRO Bank N.V.	ABN AMRO Securities (USA), Inc.	6/90
The Bank of Montreal	Nesbitt Burns Securities, Inc.	5/88
First of America Bank Corp.	First of America Securities, Inc.	10/94
First Chicago Corp.	First Chicago Capital Markets, Inc.	8/88
Minneapolis District		
Norwest Corp.	Norwest Investment Services	12/89
San Francisco District		
BankAmerica Corp.	BA Securities, Inc.	3/92
Dai-Ichi Kangyo Bank Ltd.	DKB Securities Corp.	1/91
The Sanwa Bank, Ltd.	Sanwa Securities (USA) Co., L.P.	5/90

Source: Board of Governors of the Federal Reserve System.

- Deutschebank AG
- J. P. Morgan & Company
- The Royal Bank of Canada
- Saban/Republic New York Corporation
- Swiss Bank Corporation
- The Toronto-Dominion Bank
- Dauphin Deposit Corporation

- National City Corporation
- First Union Corporation
- NationsBank Corporation
- ABN AMRO Bank NB
- The Bank of Montreal
- BankAmerica

The Toronto-Dominion Case

The most recent approval under Section 20 of the Glass-Steagall Act has been for the Toronto-Dominion Bank. Toronto-Dominion received its initial powers under Section 20 in May 1990. Under these initial powers, the subsidiary, Toronto-Dominion Securities, was authorized to underwrite and deal in certain municipal revenue bonds, mortgage-related securities, commercial paper, and asset-backed securities. The September 14, 1994, order by the Federal Reserve permitted expanded powers for the subsidiary.[4] The new powers granted to Toronto-Dominion include:

- Underwriting and dealing in, to a limited extent, all types of debt and equity securities (other than securities issued by open-end investment companies), including sovereign debt securities, corporate debt securities, convertible debt securities, debt securities issued by a trust or other vehicle secured by or representing interest in debt obligations, preferred stock, common stock, American Depositary Receipts, and other direct and indirect ownership interest in corporations and other entities ("bank-ineligible securities").
- Purchasing and selling all types of securities as a "riskless principal" on the order of customers.
- Making, acquiring, and servicing loans or other extensions of credit (including issuing letters of credit and accepting drafts) for the subsidiary's account or for the account of others.

Toronto-Dominion Securities received these powers throughout the United States. (The other operations of Toronto-Dominion Bank in the United States include a branch and limited-purpose trust company in New York City, New York; an agency in Houston, Texas; and a representative office in Chicago, Illinois.) As a result of the activities originally authorized for Toronto-Dominion Securities, the firm was, and would continue to be, a broker-dealer registered with the Securities and Exchange Commission (SEC) and a member of the National Association of Securities Dealers, Inc. (NASD). As members of the SEC and NASD, Toronto-Dominion Securities is subject to recordkeeping and reporting obligations, fiduciary standards, and other requirements of these organizations.

As a condition of the approval for new securities powers, both the bank and its security affiliate were required to demonstrate that adequate firewalls and appropriate management controls were in place. Policies and procedures covered under this provision include computer, audit, and accounting systems; internal risk management control; and necessary operational and managerial infrastructure. In addition, the Federal Reserve Board reviewed the capitalization of both Toronto-Dominion Bank and Toronto-Dominion Securities to ensure that both were properly capitalized. This determination was based both on all the facts contained in the records and on projections of the securities firm's anticipated volume in underwriting and dealing in bank-ineligible securities.

An issue associated with the Toronto-Dominion case involved the ability of the securities affiliate to offer letters of credit in connection with securities being underwritten. Previous orders of the Federal Reserve with respect to Section 20 subsidiaries include a limitation on credit enhancements by a Section 20 subsidiary that might be viewed as enhancing the creditworthiness or marketability of securities underwritten by that Section 20 subsidiary. In the case of Toronto-Dominion, apparently the request was to underwrite securities and offer credit enhancements (in the form of letters of credit) that would be associated with the underwritten securities, with the participation of other banks in the letters of credit. The Federal Reserve Board denied this request and upheld the prohibition against participating in the credit facility, even if there is participation from other commercial banks.

Another issue with respect to the Toronto-Dominion case involved the riskless principal activities. Acting as a riskless principal means that a broker-dealer may enter a transaction on its own account, which transaction is offset by an order from a client. Since the broker-dealer knows that the position will be eliminated and precisely how the position will be eliminated, the transaction is said to be one in which the broker-dealer is a riskless principal. Specifically, riskless principal is applicable to a transaction in which a broker-dealer, after receiving an order to buy (or sell) a security from a customer, purchases (or sells) the security for its own account to offset a contemporaneous sale to (or purchase from) the customer.

In the securities industry, riskless principal transactions are understood to occur in the secondary market. As such, these transactions do not constitute underwriting or dealing in securities in the primary market as relates to the powers of a Section 20 subsidiary in bank-ineligible securities transactions. Accordingly, revenue from these transactions is not included in the revenues that are limited to 10 percent of total operating revenues of the Section 20 subsidiary. However, since such transactions are considered to be secondary market transactions, Toronto-Dominion was not permitted to act as a riskless principal in selling securities on the orders of a customer that is the issuer of the securities to be sold. Nor may the Section 20 subsidiary act as a riskless principal in any transaction in which the subsidiary has a contractual agreement to place the securities as agent of the issuer. The first circumstance can be interpreted as a firm commitment underwriting arrangement, while the second is similar to a best efforts arrangement.[5]

In addition, Toronto-Dominion may not engage in securities transactions as a riskless principal for any security for which it makes a market. Nor may the affiliate represent itself as making a market in any security that it buys and sells as a riskless principal. The objective of these restrictions with respect to riskless principal activities appears to be a separation of broker-dealer activities from underwriting activities. In this sense, these provisions are similar to firewalls within the subsidiary itself.

In approving Section 20 subsidiary applications, the Federal Reserve must satisfy certain provisions of the Bank Holding Company Act.

- The proposed activities related to the making, acquiring, and servicing of loans and other extensions of credit are closely related to banking in the meaning of the act.
- The Fed must determine that the performance of the proposed activities produce benefits to the public that outweigh any possible adverse affects, such as undue concentration of resources, decreased or unfair competition, conflicts of interest, or unsound banking practices.

In the ruling for Toronto-Dominion, the Fed found that the proposed activities would not result in any significant adverse effects and that the entry of Toronto-Dominion Securities into these new areas of business would provide added convenience for customers and increase the level of competition among existing providers of these services. Thus, the benefits appear to outweigh any possible adverse effects.[6]

UNDERWRITING STOCKS

The commercial loan underwriting process can be extended in the financial evaluation of any client issuer interested in raising equity funds. The difference is that the focus shifts to the perspective of a shareholder in the underwriting scenario, as opposed to that of a commercial lender. The stockholder, whether a common stockholder or a preferred stockholder, has a claim on the issuing firm that has a lower priority than that of any debt holder. Furthermore, the claim represented by an equity security does not mature, that is, is a perpetual claim on the issuer. Thus, the analysis shifts from ability to repay over a stated time to the ability to generate cash flows indefinitely, or at least for the foreseeable future.

Preferred Stock

Preferred stock pays a level dividend; that is, the dividend does not change. An alternative term used to describe this type of equity is *preference stock*. The vast majority of preferred stock follows this model of indefinite life and fixed dividend payments. The most common exceptions are

- Limited life preferred stock with a maturity date of at least 25 years after the date of issuance.
- Money market preferred stock with a floating dividend rate that changes every 49 days. This structure is intended to ensure that the stock trades at or near par value at all times.
- Adjustable rate preferred stock pays dividends on a quarterly basis which dividends are adjusted at the same frequency. While adjustable rate issues do not mature, they may be callable at the option of the issuer.

Preferred stock may also be structured to be convertible into common stock.[7]

The value of preferred stock is based on the stream of level dividends and the rate of return to shareholders. Since the dividends associated with preferred stock do not change, preferred stock is a perpetuity. The value of a share of preferred stock is the present value of all future dividends.

$$P_0 = \left(\frac{D_1}{k} \right) \tag{1}$$

where

P_0 = Price per share
D_1 = Anticipated annual dividend per share
k = Annual rate of return to shareholder

Thus, a stock paying $2.00 per share as an annual dividend would be valued at $20.00 per share if shareholders expected a 10 percent rate of return.

In advising a client about the issuance of preferred stock, a critical element is a solid assessment of the market's perception of the riskiness of the issuer. This perception translates directly into the market's required return for the stock. The assessment of the market return can be assisted by considering several variables:

- Yield on already existing preferred stock of the issuer.
- Yield on preferred stock of a comparable firm in the industry.
- Yield on preferred stock for the industry as a whole (as available and applicable).

The amount of dividends associated with the stock must be considered as part of the fixed charges of the issuer. Projections of future cash flows must include the payment of these dividends and their impact on the financial position of the issuer.[8]

Preferred stock has the advantage for an issuer of adding to equity while not diluting the control of the firm by common shareholders. A disadvantage of this approach is that preferred stock dividends usually are fixed and represent a kind of leverage that may be disadvantageous in difficult economic conditions.

Common Stock

Common stock is a residual claim on the firm. That is, common shareholders receive dividend payments that are not fixed and in the event of liquidation have the lowest priority in any cash distribution. The order of priority is claims with a preference status (such as wages and taxes), general creditors, subordinated creditors, preferred stock, and common stock. On the other hand, common shareholders are the beneficiaries of favorable circumstances. To the extent that cash flows exceed required payments to creditors and preferred shareholders, these cash flows accrue to common shareholders and may be paid in the form of dividends or reinvested in the firm.

Dividends of common stock vary, hopefully increasing, over time. The value of common stock is, thus, the present value of these varying dividends. Operationally, it is impossible to find the present value of cash flows through infinity (which presumably a firm may pay as dividends) that vary in an unpredictable way. However, certain simplifying assumptions facilitate the process of valuation. One such assumption is that earnings, dividends, and assets grow at a constant rate of growth, g. Using this assumption, a share of common stock can be valued as follows:

$$P_0 = \left(\frac{D_1}{k - g} \right) \qquad (2)$$

where

g = Anticipated annual growth rate

In pricing the stock, these parameters will be important even if the assumption of constant growth is not realistic. Solving the model in Equation (2) for the rate of return expected by shareholders, the expected return to shareholders is comprised of dividend yield and growth rate. In the earlier preferred stock example, the projected dividend was $2 per share and shareholders required 10 percent. If the same were true, in a common stock case, ignoring the rate of growth would understate the value of the stock. If the stock was expected to grow at a 5 percent rate per year, the value of the stock would not be $20, but instead $40.[9]

In assisting a client to issue common stock, an underwriter must be attentive to each of the three factors—initial dividends, growth rate, and investor expectations with respect to rate of return. These variables and overall market conditions help ensure that the stock is issued at a price that results in a successful initial sale and strong secondary market trading.

Exchange Listing of Common Stock

For any new issue of common stock, the function of primary and secondary markets is critical. While the distribution syndicate (underwriting syndicate and selling group) prepare the issue and identify investors, the stock is actually sold through *markets*, where buyers and sellers meet to determine the public price for the securities. One of the critical functions in this process is that of *market maker*, a party that stands ready to execute buy and sell orders for customers or for its own account. A market maker takes possession of the asset traded (assuming the risk) and executes transactions at publicly quoted prices. Market makers ensure that, after the underwriting process is complete, the securities will trade in a liquid fashion. That is, investors may enter and exit the market for a given security with relative ease. These transactions take place in either organized exchanges or over-the-counter markets.

In the United States, the New York Stock Exchange (NYSE) and the American Stock Exchange (AMEX) are the national organized exchanges. In addition, the regional organized exchanges include the Midwest Exchange, the Pacific Exchange, and those in Cincinnati, Philadelphia, and Boston. The national over-the-counter (OTC) is NAS-DAQ. NASDAQ (National Association of Securities Dealers Automated Quotations) is a computerized network that links buyers and sellers through computer screens, rather than physical location. A larger number of stocks are listed on NASDAQ and an even greater number of stocks are reported without having met formal listing requirements. An investment banker should be prepared to assist its clients in deciding whether to list on a stock exchange and, if so, help select which stock exchange.

New York Stock Exchange

The NYSE is the largest and oldest stock exchange in the United States, listing securities of major U.S. corporations including the 30 firms in the Dow Jones Industrial Average. The exchange is in New York City at 11 Wall Street; often it is referred to as the Big Board. The NYSE lists approximately 1,700 stocks.

The requirements to list a stock on the NYSE are more stringent than the other alternatives. The NYSE listing requirements are contained in Exhibit 4–2. These requirements focus on the extent to which shares of a company are widely held, the size of the company, and profitability. The company must have at least 2,000 shareholders that own at least 100 shares each. Alternatively, if shareholders total 2,200, and average monthly trading volume for the most recent six months is 100,000 shares, the minimum requirement is satisfied. For an initial public offering, there must be some assurance that a minimum of 2,000 round-lot holders will own the stock. In addition, a total of no less than 1,100,000 shares must be available to the public. Market value of these public shares and net tangible assets must, at a minimum, be $18 million. Note that the primary emphasis is placed on the market value of publicly traded shares. The minimum pretax income is $2.5 million. In addition, income in the two preceding years must be at least $2 million per year. Alternatively, a firm may have a total pretax income for the last three years in the amount of $6.5 million. In this case, the most recent year must be associated with pretax income of $4.5 million. While the first pretax income requirement is aimed at a firm with a relatively consistent earnings pattern, the alternative is geared for a firm with a high recent income that may not be as consistent.

A firm that wishes to be considered for listing on the NYSE must meet the preceding quantitative listing standards. For a firm that meets these standards, the first step in the process is a review by the NYSE, on a confidential basis. NYSE reviews an applicant's case and advises whether the firm may list. Any reasons that would prevent a firm from listing also are identified during the review process. The NYSE review is at no cost to the firm. Documentation required for the review includes:

- Corporate charter and bylaws.
- Sample of stock certificates.

EXHIBIT 4–2

New York Stock Exchange: Listing Requirements

	Minimum Standards	Alternative Minimum Standards
Round-lot holders (number of holders of a unit of trading— usually 100 shares)	2,000*	Total shareholders of 2,200 and Average monthly trading volume of 100,000[†]
Public shares	1,100,000	N/A
Market value of public shares	$18,000,000	N/A
Net tangible assets	$18,000,000	N/A
Pretax income	Most recent year, $2,500,000 and Two preceding years, $2,000,000	Aggregate for last three years, $6,500,000 and Minimum in most recent year,[‡] $4,500,000

* Number of shares held by nominees or depositories is considered in addition to holders of record. In connection with initial public offerings, the NYSE will accept an undertaking that will be sold to a minimum of 2,000 round-lot holders.

† For the most recent six months.

‡ All three years must be profitable.

N/A Not applicable.

Source: *Listing Standards and Procedures for Domestic Corporations* (New York: New York Stock Exchange, October 1995).

- Annual reports to shareholders for the last three years.
- Latest available prospectus that covered a public offering, the latest SEC filings—form 10-K and interim 10-Q.
- Proxy statement for the most recent annual meeting.

- A stock distribution schedule that identifies the number of holders by the size of the holding, the 10 largest holders of record, the relationship (if any) to the company of each of the 10 largest holders, and the geographic distribution of holders.
- Recent analysts' reports, if available.
- Summary (by principal groups) of stock owned or controlled by officers, directors, and their immediate families; other concentrated holdings of 10 percent or more; and shares held under investment letters.
- Estimate of the number of nonofficer employees owning stock and total shares held.
- Number of shares held in profit sharing, savings, pension, or other similar funds or trusts established for the benefit of officers, employees, and other related parties.

If the company seeking a listing plans an initial public offering, the necessary documentation is as follows:

- Corporate charter and bylaws.
- Draft prospectus or registration statement, including financial statements.

The NYSE also has other listing requirements related to corporate governance. First, NYSE corporations must have a minimum of two outside directors. For those corporations that do not have the requisite outside directors, it is possible to appoint one at the time of listing and to have appointed the second within one year of listing. An outside director is not an employee; an officer or former officer (of the corporation or a subsidiary); a relative of a principal executive officer; or an individual acting as an advisor, consultant, or legal counsel and receiving compensation on a continuing basis in addition to director's fees.

Second, each NYSE corporation must have an audit committee. The independence of this committee is critical. The audit committee must be composed of directors completely independent of the corporation's management.

Third, an NYSE corporation must maintain the integrity of shareholder voting rights. No action may be taken that would nullify, restrict, or disparately reduce the per share voting rights of an outstanding class of common stock.

Fourth, the NYSE also is sensitive to the issue of related party transactions. Each corporation that applies for a listing on the NYSE must confirm that it will appropriately review and oversee related party transactions on an ongoing basis. Such review may be conducted by the audit committee or by a comparable body.

In essence, the requirements for listing on the NYSE involve a wide shareholder base, a substantial balance sheet, reasonable profitability, and solid internal controls.

American Stock Exchange

AMEX is the second largest exchange in the United States. This exchange lists securities of smaller firms as compared to the NYSE. AMEX also lists the stock of a number of foreign firms. Approximately 900 stocks trade on AMEX.

Exhibit 4–3 contains the listing requirements for AMEX. These are similar to the NYSE with the exception that the levels of publicly traded shares, assets, and income are lower. An applicant for listing on AMEX provides the same documents and discusses the same governance issues that are relevant to an application for NYSE listing.

NASDAQ

Until 1939, the over-the-counter market was essentially unorganized and unregulated. The Maloney Act amendments to the Securities Exchange Act permitted the creation of the National Association of Securities Dealers (NASD). The NASD is a self-regulating organization that has responsibilities in the OTC markets similar to those of organized stock markets. Stocks traded in the OTC market are separated into two classifications—those listed on NASDAQ and approximately 40,000 others. The more active stocks are listed on NASDAQ. The bids and offers of all registered market makers (dealers) of NASDAQ are shown and continu-

E X H I B I T   4-3

American Stock Exchange: Listing Requirements

	Minimum Standards	Alternative Minimum Standards
Public shareholders	(1) 800* or (2) 400 or (3) 400	(1) 800* or (2) 400 or (3) 400
Public shares	(1) 500,000 or (2) 1 million or (3) 500,000, with daily trading volume of at least 2,000 shares[†]	(1) 500,000 or (2) 1 million or (3) 500,000, with daily trading volume of at least 2,000 shares[†]
Market value of public shares	$3,000,000	$15,000,000
Minimum price per share	$3	$3
Shareholders' equity	$4,000,000	$4,000,000
Pretax income	Most recent year or two of the last three years, $750,000	At least a three-year operating history (No income requirements)

* Exclusive of the holdings of officers, directors, controlling shareholders, and other concentrated family holdings.
† For prior six months.
Source: American Stock Exchange, 1995.

ously updated on this market's automated system. This makes it possible for a broker or a customer to identify the best price being quoted. Since any NASDAQ market dealer can be a market maker in any security simply by notifying NASDAQ of its intentions, an average of 11 market makers exist for each security traded on NASDAQ. Until recently, the 40,000 stocks that were not actually listed on NASDAQ were quoted on a daily basis through printed media, or Pink Sheets. Beginning in June 1990, this information has appeared on an electronic bulletin board on which the dealers may post and update quotes.

The bulletin board should not be confused with the NASDAQ system. There are several differences.

- NASDAQ has specific minimum listing requirements, while the bulletin board does not. NASDAQ quotations are firm dealer commitments that are not required for the bulletin board. Furthermore, dealers may even post indications of interest without including a price.
- NASDAQ transmits information to wire services and to information service vendors; the bulletin board does not.
- NASDAQ is a telephone market supported by a computer system for quotation and execution of orders. Quotations are managed via leased telephone lines from the NASDAQ Central Processing Complex with collection and dissemination to dealers' desktop computer terminals.

Stocks listed on NASDAQ are either National Market System (NMS) or second-tier stocks. NMS stocks are the most widely held and actively traded among the NASDAQ listed stocks and number approximately 3,000. For NMS stocks, OTC dealers must provide information about the last sale within 90 seconds of that trade. For second-tier stocks, dealers must report only the aggregate trading volume at the end of each trading day. NASDAQ now has the second greatest trading volume in the United States, second only to the NYSE.

Exhibit 4–4 includes the minimum listing requirements for NASDAQ. There are two alternatives to obtain a NASDAQ listing. Alternative 1 places more emphasis on the operating results of the issuer in recent years and less emphasis on the size of the organization. On the other hand, Alternative 2 places more emphasis on market

E X H I B I T   4–4

NASDAQ: Listing Requirements

	Alternative 1	Alternative 2
Registration under Section 12(g) of the Securities Exchange Act of 1934 or equivalent	Yes	Yes
Net tangible assets*	$4 million	$12 million
Net income (in latest fiscal year or two of the last three fiscal years)	$400,000	N/A
Pretax income (in latest fiscal year or two of the last three fiscal years)	$750,000	N/A
Public float (shares)†	500,000	1 million
Market value of float	$3 million	$15 million
Operating history	N/A	3 years
Minimum bid price	$5	$3
Shareholders:		
If between 0.5 and 1 million shares publicly held	800	400
If more than 1 million shares publicly held	400	400
If more than 0.5 million shares held and average daily volume in excess of 2,000 shares	400	400
Number of market makers	2	2

* Net tangible assets equal total assets minus intangible assets minus liabilities.

† Those shares not "held directly or indirectly by any officer or director of the issuer and by any person who is the beneficial owner of more than 10 percent of the total shares outstanding."

N/A not applicable.

Source: *The NASDAQ Stock Market Listing Application* (New York: The NASDAQ Stock Market, Inc., October 1995).

capitalization and the strength of the firm's balance sheet.[10] Under both alternatives, the firm must be registered under the Securities Exchange Act of 1934. For Alternative 1, net tangible assets (net assets less intangible assets) must be at least $4 million with net income and pretax income of at least $400,000 and $750,000 in the latest year or in two of the last three years. Alternative 2 has no income requirements but net tangible assets must be at least $12 million. Under Alternative 1, no operating history is required while Alternative 2 requires a three-year operating history.

Alternative 2 places a greater emphasis on the market value of outstanding shares. There must be a public float of at least 1 million shares and a value of at least $15 million. The public float represents shares not held by insiders which is defined as not being held directly or indirectly by any officer or director. Furthermore, the public float does not include shares held by anyone with more than a 10 percent ownership stake in the issuer. On the other hand, Alternative 1 requires a public float of only 500,000 shares with a market value of $3 million. The minimum bid price for stock under Alternative 1 must be $5 while Alternative 2 requires a minimum $3.

Essentially, the number of shareholders is the same under both alternatives. To be listed, a firm must have at least 400 shareholders. The only exception is under Alternative 1. If the firm has between 500,000 and 1 million publicly traded shares, the minimum number of shareholders is 800. It is possible for this minimum requirement to be relaxed as well. Under Alternative 1, if more than 500,000 shares are publicly held and the average daily volume of trading in the stock exceeds 2,000 shares, the minimum number of shareholders drops back to 400.

In both cases, the listing firm must have market makers in place. The minimum number of market makers is two. However, because every dealer registered with NASDAQ can become a market maker and the average number of market makers is 11 per security, this requirement is not a binding constraint.

A firm that does not qualify for listing as a NMS stock may qualify for listing in the NASDAQ SmallCap market. Exhibit 4–5 summarizes these requirements. Although registration under the Securities Exchange Act of 1934 is required, there is temporary, automatic exemption for initial public offerings (IPOs). Unadjusted shareholders' equity must be at least $2 million, one-half the required minimum for net tangible assets under Alternative 1 for a

EXHIBIT 4-5

NASDAQ: SmallCap Listing Requirements

	SmallCap
Registration under Section 12(g) of the Securities Exchange Act of 1934 or equivalent*	Yes
Total shareholders' equity	$2 million
Net income (in latest fiscal year or two of the last three fiscal years)	N/A
Pretax income (in latest fiscal year or two of the last three fiscal years)	N/A
Public float (shares)†	100,000
Market value of float	$1 million
Operating history	N/A
Minimum bid price	$3
Shareholders	300
Number of market makers	2
Total assets	$4 million

* A temporary, automatic exemption exists for initial public offerings.

† Those shares not "held directly or indirectly by any officer or director of the issuer and by any person who is the beneficial owner of more than 10 percent of the total shares outstanding."

N/A not applicable.

Source: *The NASDAQ Stock Market Listing Application* (New York: The NASDAQ Stock Market, Inc., October 1995).

NMS stock. There is no requirement with respect to net income, pretax income, or operating history. The public float must be at least 100,000 shares, with a market value of at least $1 million.

Other minimum requirements are similar to those associated with Alternatives 1 and 2. The minimum bid price for a share of stock to be listed is $3; the minimum number of shareholders is 300; and the minimum number of market makers is two.

A SmallCap listing has one requirement not included in the other alternatives. Total assets must amount to $4 million. This requirement, together with a $2 million minimum, suggests a firm listing at the margin must have a debt ratio of no more than 50 percent.

Stock Exchange Listing Fees

In addition to meeting requirements with respect to financial and market position, firms listing their stock in either of these markets must pay listing fees.[11] Exhibit 4–6 is a summary of the fees for listing on the NYSE, AMEX, NASDAQ National Market, and NASDAQ SmallCap. The minimum listing charge for NYSE is $51,550. For AMEX and NASDAQ, the minimum is $10,000 or less. The maximum fee NYSE requires is $767,100 for a listing of 200 million shares. This schedule continues to increase for listings in excess of 200 million shares. On the other hand, AMEX and NASDAQ National Market have maximum fees of $50,000. A SmallCap issue has a maximum listing fee of $10,000.

An issuer of common stock has a wide range of alternatives when deciding whether to list on an organized exchange or in the OTC market. An investment banker should be prepared to assist a client in analyzing both the costs and benefits of such a listing. Additional information that should be considered is the type of industry in which the issuing firm is engaged and the extent to which similar firms are traded either OTC or in organized exchanges. Another consideration for the decision to list is the investor market to which the issuer would like to appeal. If the company is of national interest, or potentially national interest, a national organized exchange or a NASDAQ National Market listing may be appropriate. On the other hand, if the stock is of primarily regional interest, listing on a regional exchange makes much more logistic sense and is probably more efficient in terms of listing expense.

UNDERWRITING CORPORATE BONDS

Corporate bonds in the United States may be issued by a number of entities—utilities, transportation firms, industrial companies, and financial institutions. Among the classification of industrials, a wide range of companies are represented, including manufacturing firms, retail organizations, and service companies. Accordingly, the characteristics of a bond issued in the corporate sector is influenced

EXHIBIT 4-6

Listing Fees of NYSE, AMEX, and NASDAQ

Shares (millions)	NYSE* ($)	AMEX† ($)	NASDAQ National Market ($)‡	NASDAQ SmallCap ($)§
Up to 1	51,550	10,000	5,000 to 10,000	6,000
1+ to 2	51,550+ to 66,300	15,000	10,000+ to 15,000	6,000+ to 7,000
2+ to 3	66,300+ to 73,700	20,000	15,000+ to 20,000	7,000+ to 8,000
3+ to 4	73,700+ to 81,100	22,500	20,000+ to 25,000	8,000+ to 9,000
4+ to 5	81,100+ to 84,600	25,000	25,000+ to 30,000	9,000+ to 10,000
5+ to 6	84,600+ to 88,100	27,500	30,000+ to 32,500	10,000
6+ to 7	88,100+ to 91,600	30,000	32,500+ to 35,000	10,000
7+ to 8	91,600+ to 95,100	32,500	35,000+ to 37,500	10,000
8+ to 9	95,100+ to 98,600	35,000	37,500+ to 40,000	10,000
9+ to 10	98,600+ to 102,100	37,500	40,000+ to 42,500	10,000
10+ to 11	102,100+ to 105,600	42,500	42,500+ to 45,000	10,000
11+ to 12	105,600+ to 109,100	42,500	45,000+ to 47,500	10,000
12+ to 13	109,100+ to 112,600	42,500	47,500+ to 50,000	10,000
13+ to 14	112,600+ to 116,100	42,500	50,000	10,000
14+ to 15	116,100+ to 119,600	42,500	50,000	10,000
15+ to 20	119,600+ to 137,100	50,000	50,000	10,000
20+ to 25	137,100+ to 154,600	50,000	50,000	10,000

Continued

25+ to 50	154,600+ to 242,100	50,000	10,000
50+ to 75	242,100+ to 329,600	50,000	10,000
75+ to 100	329,600+ to 417,100	50,000	10,000
100+ to 200	417,100+ to 767,100	50,000	10,000
Maximum	=	50,000	10,000

* Includes a one-time initial listing charge of $36,800.

† Includes a one-time initial listing charge of $5,000.

‡ Consists of a one-time fee and variable fees per share up to a maximum of $50,000:
- $5,000 one-time fee
- Variable fee schedule per each class of security:

Tier	Number of Shares Outstanding	Fee per share
1	1 to 5,000,000	$0.005—less than 5 million
2	5,000,001 to 15,000,000	0.0025—more than 5 million
3	15,000,001 +	0.001

For issues exceeding 5 million shares, only those shares over 5 million are billed at $0.0025. Similarly, for issues exceeding 15 million, only those shares over 15 million are billed at $0.001. Maximum entry fees to be paid per issuer (covering all classes of securities) cannot exceed $50,000, inclusive of the $5,000 original company listing.

§ Consists of a one-time fee and variable fees per share up to a maximum of $10,000:
- $5,000 one-time company listing fee.
- Variable fee schedule per each class of security:
  - a. Equity securities—the greater of $1,000 or $0.01/share, not to exceed $5,000.
  - b. Convertible debentures—the greater of $1,000 or $50 per million dollars face value of debentures, not to exceed $5,000.

Maximum entry fees to be paid per issuer cannot exceed $10,000, inclusive of $5,000 original company listing fee.

‖ $767,100 plus $0.0035 times shares from 200 million to 300 million plus $0.0019 times shares above 300 million.

Sources: American Stock Exchange, New York Stock Exchange, and NASDAQ National Market, October 1995, unpublished data.

99

by the industry in which the issuer participates. However, the general characteristics and considerations contained in this section apply regardless of a specific industry.

The document containing the terms of a bond issue and the rights of bondholders is an *indenture*. This agreement specifies the form of a bond being offered for sale; interest to be paid; maturity date of the issue; call provisions and protective covenants, if any; collateral pledged; repayment schedule; and any other terms relevant to the issue. Under the Trust Indenture Act of 1939 that amended the Securities Act of 1933, bond issuers must specify a corporation that will administer the terms of the indenture. This corporation, the *trustee*, must be free of any conflict of interest and is responsible for making semiannual disclosures of relevant information to bondholders. This act prohibits impairment of bondholders' right to sue individually and requires the trustee to make it possible for bondholders to communicate with each other by providing a list of bondholders. Municipal bond issuers are exempted from this federal law because they are not subject to most federal securities regulations.

Types of Bonds

A bond may be a *registered bond* or a *bearer bond*. A registered bond is one whose owner's name is recorded by the issuer or its transfer agent. A *transfer agent* is generally a commercial bank that issues, registers, and redeems bonds on behalf of the issuer. In this function, a transfer agent maintains records of changes in ownership, cancels old bond certificates, updates records when new bonds are sold, and ensures that new offerings of bonds are not overissued. For bond issues, the transfer agent also may be referred to as a registrar. Under provisions of the Trust Indenture Act of 1939, the trustee has a responsibility of ensuring that interest payments are made to registered bondholders.

A bearer bond is payable to the holder of the bond, rather than to a registered owner on the records of a transfer agent or registrar. For bearer bonds, there is no record of ownership. Title is held by anyone who possesses the security and holds it in good faith. Bond interest generally is paid semiannually when detachable coupons are clipped and mailed to a bank for collection. Thus, these bond coupons are collected in much the same way as checks.

Bonds also may be distinguished by the structure of their maturity dates. *Term bonds* have a single maturity date while serial bonds are issued as a set of bonds each having a specific maturity date. Interest is paid during the life of the term bond and the principal is repaid on maturity. Term bonds may have *sinking fund provisions*. Sinking fund requirements obligate bond issuers to retire the outstanding bonds according to a predetermined schedule, regardless of market conditions. Some sinking fund requirements may be satisfied by redeeming (calling) a certain number of bonds per year. Other sinking fund requirements may be satisfied by purchasing bonds in the open market.

On the other hand, *serial bonds* enable the issuer to spread the maturities over a predetermined schedule. These bonds are commonly used by states and municipal governments. For example, bonds may be issued at six-month intervals over several years; each bond has its own maturity date that is predetermined at the time of the initial offering.

Bonds also may be distinguished by their original maturity. Corporate borrowings with an initial maturity of 20 to 30 years are referred to as *bonds* while those with an initial maturity of less than 10 years are frequently referred to as *notes*.[12]

Corporate bonds may also be distinguished by the collateral associated with an issue. A *mortgage bond* is secured either by real property (established by a mortgage) or personal property of the issuer. Holders of mortgage bonds have a lien against the assets that are pledged. In the event of a default, the pledged assets may be sold to satisfy the obligations. In practice, this is rarely done. When necessary, plans of reorganization are structured to avoid the need to sell the collateral. *Collateral trust bonds* are issued by holding companies with the stock of their subsidiaries as their collateral. *Equipment trust certificates* are issued by a bond trustee to finance the purchase of major pieces of transportation equipment that are then leased to the issuer of the bonds. Lease payments pay interest and principal to holders of the equipment trust certificates. This form of financing was initiated by the railroad industry; now it is commonly used by trucking companies to acquire large fleets of trucks, by airlines to purchase aircraft, and by international oil companies to buy tankers.

When there is no collateral for bonds, they are referred to as debentures. Holders of debentures have the same claim as general creditors; that is, no assets are pledged specifically to secure the debt. *Subordinated debentures* are associated with a claim having a lower priority than that of general creditors. Holders of subordinated debentures receive no cash distributions (ongoing or on liquidation) until the claims of securities to which the debentures are subordinated have been fully satisfied.

Guaranteed bonds are an issuer's bonds that have principal and interest guaranteed by a third party. Thus, a holder of a guaranteed bond may look to both the issuer and the guarantor to satisfy the terms of the indenture.

Like some preferred stock, some bonds are *convertible*. A conversion provision entitles the bondholder to convert the bond into common stock of the bond issuer. *Exchangeable bonds* permit the bondholder to exchange the bonds for common stock of a company other than the issuer of the bond. Some corporate bonds are issued with *warrants*. A warrant is similar to an option, in that it entitles the holder to purchase common stock of the issuer of the debt or common stock of a firm other than the issuer. A warrant may even entitle the holder to purchase another debt obligation of the issuer. Generally, warrants are detachable and may be sold separately in the market. A warrant is similar to a call option that is embedded in the provisions of the bond.

Another form of embedded option is that of a *putable bond*. Here the bondholder has the right to sell the bond back to the issuer at par on dates specified in the indenture. The effect of a putable bond is to maintain the market value of the bond close to the strike price or par.

Bonds also may be classified by the method of interest payment. Typically, interest is set by the coupon rate designated in the indenture. If no interest is paid until maturity, the bond is a *zero-coupon* bond. The market value of a zero-coupon bond is always less than par; that is, the present value of the maturity value.

When interest is paid but allowed to vary, the bond is said to have a *floating-rate* coupon. The coupon is reset periodically according to a specified benchmark. Floating-rate bonds are attractive to some institutional investors because the cash flow stream associated with the bonds may more closely match the cash flows of the investors' liabilities. As long as the credit quality of the issuer remains constant, a floating-rate bond sells at or near par value. This is true because the interest payments associated with the bond adjust when market interest rates adjust. If the spread over the index or reference rate used is adequate at the time of issue, it also will be adequate after adjustment to prevailing market interest rates on reset dates. However, if the credit quality of the issuer deteriorates in the interim, this spread over the index or reference rate may be insufficient to adequately compensate bondholders for the perceived higher risk associated with the issuer. In such a case, the bond sells at a discount. Floating-rate issues also may be associated with put options, be exchangeable at the option of the issuer into another fixed-rate security, or convertible into common stock of the issuer at the option of the bondholder. Some corporate issues also have interest-rate caps and floors.[13]

When bond issuers have less than investment grade credit ratings, the bonds are referred to as *junk bonds*. (The following section discusses bond credit ratings.) Junk bonds issued in connection with leveraged buyouts or recapitalizations frequently have special provisions for the payment of interest. Among these are

- Deferred-interest bonds.
- Step-up bonds.
- Payment-in-kind bonds.

Deferred-interest bonds permit the issuers to forgo payment of interest for a specified time, usually three to seven years. After this time, interest is paid as usual. Because of the long period for which interest is not payable, such bonds sell at a discount. *Step-up bonds* pay interest from the date of issue to the date of maturity. However, the coupon rate in the early periods is lower than the coupon rate that will be paid in the latter part of the bond's life. Thus, the coupon steps up to a higher coupon rate. The issuer of *payment-in-kind bonds* has an option to either make cash payments or give the bond-holder another bond. The new bond would be similar as it would have the same coupon rate and a par value equal to the amount of interest that would otherwise have been paid. In most cases, the issuer has this option for 5 to 10 years.

A recent innovation in the bond market is the introduction of the *medium-term note* (MTN) introduced by Merrill Lynch in 1981. The purpose was to offer an alternative debt instrument with a term somewhere between commercial paper and long-term bonds.[14] The first MTN issue underwritten by Merrill Lynch was for Ford Motor Credit Company. By 1983, however, GMAC and Chrysler Financial also had retained Merrill Lynch to act as their agent in the issuance of MTNs. The primary issuers of MTNs are finance companies, banks, bank holding companies, industrial firms, utilities, sovereign governments, and government agencies. MTNs are issued by highly creditworthy companies and the maturities are five years or less. Typically, the rating for MTNs corresponds to the rating of other debt issued. For example, unsecured MTNs carry the same credit rating as an issuer's long-term unsecured bonds while secured MTNs carry the same credit rating as the issuer's secured bonds.

Several types of MTNs may be issued:

- Fixed-rate MTNs—semiannual interest, 30/360-day basis, with an appropriate spread over a comparable Treasury security.

- Floating-rate MTNs—monthly, quarterly, or semi-annually reset periods, using an index or reference rate such as LIBOR, commercial paper rate, Treasury bills, or the prime rate.
- Credit-supported MTNs—backed by an irrevocable letter of credit or other guarantee.
- Collateralized MTNs—used primarily by thrifts with mortgage-backed securities as collateral.
- Amortizing MTNs—structured much like an amortizing automobile loan or mortgage.
- Multicurrency MTN—paid in U.S. dollars based on the exchange rate of 1 of 10 different foreign currencies.

The type of instrument selected for debt issuance depends on the funding requirements of the issuer. An investment banker should be prepared to discuss all possible alternatives with its client.

Bond Ratings

The cost of a debt issuance for the client of an investment banker depends, among other things, on the issuer's credit rating. Credit ratings for bonds are obtained through one of several rating agencies. The most widely used are Standard & Poor's (S&P) and Moody's Investors Service. S&P is a subsidiary of McGraw-Hill Companies and supplies debt ratings for asset-backed securities, corporate and municipal bonds, commercial paper, common stock, and preferred stock. Moody's—a subsidiary of Dun & Bradstreet, Inc.—rates commercial paper, bonds, and short-term tax-exempt notes of states and municipalities. The two rating agencies use similar systems in their description of creditworthiness. S&P uses the following rating categories:

- AAA—highest rating, suggesting extremely strong ability to pay principal and interest.
- AA—high-quality issuance with very strong repayment capacity, differing from AAA only by a small degree.

- A—strong capacity to pay principal and interest but somewhat more susceptible to adverse economic conditions.
- BBB—adequate capacity to pay principal and interest but more susceptible to adverse economic conditions than firms in the A category.
- BB, B, CCC, CC—ability to pay principal and interest is to a greater or lesser degree speculative with BB the least speculative and CC the most speculative.
- C—inability to pay interest on an income bond.[15]
- D—in default, principal and/or interest in arrears.

Ratings are based on quantitative and qualitative criteria. Basic quantitative considerations include the firm's debt and its debt-servicing capacity.[16] Structural aspects of the bond issue are also applicable, including mortgage subordination and guarantee provisions, sinking fund provisions, and maturity. Factors relevant to the firm's particular operating environment may include sales stability, labor relations, resource availability, political risk exposure in overseas operation, and unfunded pension liabilities. Government regulatory and environmental protection issues also are considered in this evaluation.

Bonds rated AAA through BBB are considered *investment grade* securities. From the issuer's perspective, the higher the bond rating, the lower the interest rate required by investors. Accordingly, firms are careful to protect their bond ratings.

Once an issue has been rated, the next step is to attach an appropriate coupon rate or yield to it. This is best accomplished by determining the current spread over Treasuries or other index rates in the market of similarly rated bonds. Of course, the comparison must be for similar maturities. Ultimately, the market will be the final judge as to the appropriateness of the yield. Accordingly, an investment banker must be prepared to monitor market conditions and the responsiveness of potential investors to the deal as it is being structured.

UNDERWRITING MUNICIPAL REVENUE BONDS

Underwriters of municipal revenue bonds follow the same process with disclosure and pricing as described in Chapter 3. However, the underwriting process includes considerations particular to the type of revenue bond being issued. The following is an example of credit and other considerations relevant in one type of municipal revenue bond.

Electric Utility Bonds

Until recently, electric utilities enjoyed essentially a monopoly status. Today, there is much more competition to supply the essential electricity for a city or other political subdivision. *Municipal utilities* are owned and/or operated by municipalities and state agencies to provide service to the general public. These relatively small utilities serve approximately 15 percent of the U.S. population, although municipal systems account for more than 60 percent of the utility companies. *Investor-owned utilities* are organized as tax-paying, profit-oriented businesses owned by shareholders. Essentially, investor-owned utilities have a franchise to serve their specific areas according to state and/or federal regulations. These utilities generate approximately 76 percent of all the power used by ultimate consumers. *Rural electric cooperatives* are nonprofit, customer-owned electric utilities that distribute power in primarily rural areas. These cooperatives account for approximately 7.5 percent of the power used by ultimate consumers. *Federal power agencies* are mostly wholesale utilities that sell their power to other utilities (usually cooperatives and municipal utilities) rather than to ultimate consumers.

In analyzing an electric utility, some of the issues that should be addressed are

- *Regulatory environment.* Can the utility set its own rates and issue debt as needed? If not, what is the recent history of obtaining rate relief?

- *Competitive position.* Are rates comparable to those of other utilities in the area, especially industrial rates? Compare projections for rate increases for both the utility being evaluated and its competitors.
- *Nuclear exposure.* Does the utility have nuclear facilities? If so, what is the recent operating history?
- *Capital requirements.* What are the capital requirements? How will they be financed? Is the debt short term or long term?
- *Fuel mix and asset concentration.* Is the mix of fuel diversified to guard against unexpected price fluctuations?
- *Excess capacity margin.* If there is excess capacity, can the utility make profitable off-system sales?
- *Financial position.* What is the ability of the utility to service debt? Coverage ratios are appropriate statistical techniques in this area.
- *Economics and demographics.* Ideally, the utility should service areas of modest growth. If the growth rate is exceptionally high, the utility may have trouble meeting its servicing obligations. If the growth rate is low, the utility may have trouble meeting its financial obligations.
- *Customer mix.* A high percentage of residential customers is preferable to a high percentage of industrial customers because residential customers change consumption patterns more slowly than industrial customers. The presence of a large industrial load suggests potential volatility of demand and revenue.
- *Management focus.* Is management concentrating on important issues such as cost cutting, conservation, marketing power outside the traditional service area?

Clearly, these factors are related both to the internal condition of the electric utility and its external environment. Financial analysis of a potential revenue bond must include issues specific to the industry of the issuer and its competition position.

Other Issuers

Other issuers of municipal revenue bonds have varied functions and the relevant factors vary considerably. Examples are water and sewer systems, hospitals, academic medical centers, health maintenance organizations, colleges and universities, airports, pollution control projects, and industrial development projects.

THE NEED FOR INDUSTRY EXPERTISE

Regardless of the type of instrument being underwritten—corporate stock, corporate bonds, or municipal revenue bonds—it is clear that an investment banker must have an appreciation for the industry of the issuer and the market in which the securities will be sold. Commercial lending experience can be indispensable in this regard. Also, the client relationships built through the commercial lending process can help cultivate investment banking relationships between medium-size firms that are not particularly well served by other investment bankers. With appropriate market intelligence, a Section 20 subsidiary can capture a significant part of this market.

SELECTED REFERENCES

Committee on Banking, Finance, and Urban Affairs. *Compilation of Basic Banking Laws.* Washington, DC: US Government Printing Office, 1992.

Fabozzi, Frank J. *Bond Markets, Analysis and Strategies.* 2nd ed. Englewood Cliffs, NJ: Prentice Hall, 1993.

Fitch, Thomas. *Dictionary of Banking Terms.* Hauppauge, NY: Barron's Educational Series, 1990.

Johnson, Hazel J. *Financial Institutions and Markets: A Global Perspective.* New York: McGraw-Hill, 1993.

Krellenstein, Gary M. "Tax-Exempt Electric Utility Debt." In *The Handbook of Municipal Bonds,* ed. Susan C. Heide, Robert A. Klein, and Jess Lederman. Chicago: Probus Publishing Company, 1994.

Listing Standards and Procedures for Domestic Corporations. New York: New York Stock Exchange, 1995.

The NASDAQ Stock Market Listing Application. New York: NASDAQ, 1995.

Office of Technology Assessment, Congress of the United States. *Electronic Bulls and Bears.* Washington, DC: U.S. Government Printing Office, 1990.

ENDNOTES

1. See also Chapters 1 and 3 for a discussion of this legislation.
2. See Banking Act of 1933 in Committee on Banking, Finance, and Urban Affairs, *Compilation of Basic Banking Laws* (Washington, DC: U.S. Government Printing Office, 1992).
3. In the second half of 1995, Chase Manhattan Corporation and Chemical Banking Corporation merged. The new institution retained the Chase Manhattan name.
4. See *Federal Reserve Bulletin*, November 1994.
5. See Chapter 2 for a discussion of these underwriting arrangements.
6. Also note that the Federal Reserve has offered an alternative index revenue test that measures compliance with the 10 percent limitation. A bank applying for a Section 20 subsidiary authorization may elect either of the two approaches. Description of this method may be found in *Order Approving Modifications to the Section 20 Orders*, 75 *Federal Reserve Bulletin* 751 (1989), *Order Approving Modifications to the Section 20 Orders*, 79 *Federal Reserve Bulletin* 226 (1993) and *Supple-*

ment to Order Approving Modifications to Section 20 Orders, 79 *Federal Reserve Bulletin* 360 (1993).

7. See also Chapter 2 for discussion of equity versus debt issues.

8. See Equation 3 in Chapter 2 for the fixed-charge-coverage ratio. Because preferred stock dividends are paid on an after-tax basis, their inclusion in the denominator of the ratio requires that total preferred stock dividends be grossed up by dividing the amount by the quantity $(1 - t)$.

9.
$$P_0 = \frac{\$2}{(.10 - .05)} = \$40$$

10. Market capitalization is the total market value of equity, as measured by the product of total shares outstanding and price per share.

11. There are also annual fees for continued listing. The composition of listing fees is a one-time charge plus fees directly related to the number of shares issued.

12. Treasury securities with original maturities of 2 to 10 years also are referred to as notes. See also Chapter 3.

13. See Chapter 2 for the use of derivatives to manage interest rate risk.

14. The MTN was introduced as a direct form of financing by GMAC in 1972 to fund automobile loans with maturities of five years or less. The 1972 introduction was sold directly to investors, with no agent or underwriter.

15. An income bond pays interest only if the issuing firm earns sufficient income.

16. See Chapter 2 for a discussion of debt-servicing capacity.

CHAPTER 5

Asset-Backed Securities

INTRODUCTION

Asset-backed securities are primarily debt securities collateralized by specific financial assets. The most prevalent financial asset used for this purpose is the residential mortgage. However, the market is expanding rapidly and now includes automobile loans, credit cards, and commercial loans. This segment of the securities industry is important for commercial banks for two reasons:

- Commercial banks originate many of the financial assets that form the basis for asset-backed securities.
- As the trend continues toward securitization, commercial banks can expect to realize significant revenues by bringing asset-backed securities to market as underwriters.

As is true in other segments of the securities industry, the skills developed by commercial lending officers and investment portfolio managers in the context of the commercial banking industry transfer to the arena of asset-backed securities. The additional skills required are in large measure packaging skills; that is, the key is combining the right assets with appropriate cash flows to make securitized assets attractive to the investing public. In addition, underwriting asset-backed securities requires an appreciation for financial engineering in the sense that cash flows of the underlying assets sometimes must be modified to make the resulting security more marketable.

THE NATURE OF ASSET-BACKED SECURITIES

An asset-backed security is one that is collateralized, in some way, by other financial assets, usually loans. In essence, (1) loans are removed from the balance sheet of the issuer and (2) interests in the pool of loans are sold to investors. As a result, the issuer is able to become more liquid and originate even more loans. Typically, the issuer of asset-backed securities continues to accept payments, send statements, and perform other functions to service the loans. For these activities, the issuer of asset-backed securities is paid a fee, generally 50 basis points of the unpaid balance. The process of converting loans (and other financial assets) into securities sold to investors is *securitization*.

The form of securitized assets varies. Generally, there are three basic categories:

1. Pass-through securities.
2. Asset-backed bonds.
3. Pay-through bonds.

Pass-Through Securities

Pass-through securities pay investors their proportional shares of cash flows generated by underlying assets. These cash flows include both principal and interest payments. A fee for servicing the underlying assets is deducted from each interest payment. A pass-through security represents ownership in a pool of assets. The assets are removed from the balance sheet of the originator of the loans and placed in a *trust*. In turn, the trust issues certificates of ownership to investors, the effective owners of the underlying assets.

Because the assets in the pool are typically mortgage loans and consumer receivables (automobile loans and credit card receivables), payments on the loans are generated monthly. All cash flows, with the exception of the servicing fee, flow to investors. These payments include interest, principal, and any prepayments of principal. Thus, cash flows from the underlying assets are said to be dedicated cash flows.

Asset-Backed Bonds

Asset-backed bonds remain on the balance sheet of the issuer. Underlying assets collateralize the bonds and also remain on the balance sheet of the issuer. The underlying assets may be loans or pass-through securities. As is true with other types of bonds, interest is paid semiannually and the face amount (par value or maturity value) is paid on maturity. One frequent characteristic of asset-backed bonds is that they are typically overcollateralized; that is, the value of underlying assets is greater than the face value of asset-backed bonds. Each quarter, the value of the underlying assets (collateral) is assessed. If this amount is less than the amount specified in the bond indenture, additional loans or pass-through securities must be added to the collateral.

Unlike pass-through securities, asset-backed bonds do not have dedicated cash flows from the underlying assets. Also, because assets remain on the balance sheet of the issuer, no trust is formed.

Pay-Through Bonds

Pay-through bonds are a hybrid of pass-through securities and asset-backed bonds. Pay-through bonds are obligations of the issuer, as are asset-backed bonds. However, all cash flows are dedicated to servicing the obligation represented by pay-through bonds and a separate entity is formed to hold the underlying assets, as with pass-through securities. This separate entity also issues the bonds. Interest and principal payments are made monthly or quarterly.

Unlike either pass-through securities or asset-backed bonds, pay-through bonds are issued in different *tranches*. An *accrual* or *accretion bond* is similar to a zero-coupon bond and frequently referred to as a *Z-bond*. This tranche receives no interest or principal until it matures. Other tranches receive payments of interest at regular intervals. Commonly, only one tranche receives principal payments at a time. When principal has been repaid for the first tranche, then the second tranche begins to receive principal payments. When the second tranche has been completely repaid with respect to principal, the third tranche begins to receive principal payments.

This structure is intended to eliminate much of the uncertainty with respect to *prepayment risk*. Prepayment risk is the exposure that a long-term investor faces when purchasing an amortizing security that is repaid much earlier than the original maturity date. Despite the investor's gain on the early return of principal, the anticipated stream of interest payments can be drastically reduced. Pay-through bonds give investors relatively more control over this eventuality. Pay-through bonds also may contain a residual tranche that receives cash flows in excess of the obligations to the other tranches. This may occur, for example, when the rate of prepayment anticipated at the time of securitization exceeds the actual, realized rate of prepayment. Then, total interest payments are greater than they would have been. These excess interest payments accrue to the residual tranche investor.

A Comparison

Exhibit 5–1 provides a summary of the characteristics of the three types of securities. (These general characteristics may differ considerably in actual application.) Pass-through securities represent the first generation of asset-

EXHIBIT 5-1

Types of Asset-Backed Securities

	Pass-Through Securities	Asset-Backed Bonds	Pay-Through Bonds
Payment frequency	Monthly	Semiannually	Monthly or Quarterly
Recorded on the balance sheet of the issuer?	No	Yes	No
Cash flows from underlying assets dedicated to investors?	Yes	No	Yes
Trust or other separate entity created?	Yes	No	Yes
Classes of securities	Same for all investors	Same for all investors	Different tranches within one issue

backed securities. Pay-through bonds are the most recent innovation in the field and are decidedly more complex. An investment banker must have a full appreciation for the financial structures necessary for each type to advise clients interested in securitization. All three types offer the advantage of an alternative funding source that can be tapped relatively easily. Another advantage of these asset-backed securities is that the credit rating of the certificates or bonds are determined to a great extent by the creditworthiness of the underlying assets rather than the creditworthiness of the issuer.

Note that government agencies have had a major role in the development of the asset-backed securities market, having introduced pass-through securities in the 1970s. These initial issuances of mortgage-backed pass-throughs have been followed by private sector issues and innovation in underlying assets that now include automobile loans, credit card receivables, commercial loans, computer and truck leases, loans for mobile homes, and other trade receivables.

In addition, commercial paper and preferred stock have been issued with asset backing. Usually, commercial paper is secured by credit card receivables, automobile and utility leases, and trade receivables. Preferred stock is frequently secured by mortgage-backed securities and trade receivables. Both asset-backed commercial paper and preferred stock have interest or dividend payments that are not tied to the cash flows of the *underlying* assets.

For *asset-backed preferred stock*, the dividend is auction rated. The dividends on this stock are paid and adjusted quarterly. These instruments have been issued by commercial bank holding companies since 1982 and pay interest based on a spread over Treasury rates. Because of this frequent change in the dividend rate, the market price of this preferred stock remains very close to par value. These adjustable-rate issues have no maturity date and often may be called at the option of the issuer.

With respect to *asset-backed commercial paper*, these programs typically do not unwind when underlying assets amortize. Instead, new receivables are bought continually, with the net effect that commercial paper is rolled over when it matures. There are a number of other differences between asset-backed commercial paper and the instruments described in Exhibit 5–1:

- Commercial paper is issued to purchase underlying assets, not to facilitate their sale.
- Investment bankers typically provide credit enhancements or guarantees for asset-backed commercial paper.
- In other cases, credit enhancement is typically provided by a third party.
- While mortgage-backed securities are relatively liquid, asset-backed commercial paper is much less liquid because there is no active secondary market.

Commercial banks involved in facilitating the issuance of asset-backed commercial paper perform credit analyses very similar to normal commercial lending practice. The pool of receivables or other assets is evaluated and, after purchase, monitored to ensure that creditworthiness is maintained.

THE BENEFITS AND COSTS OF SECURITIZATION

Securitization provides a number of advantages for corporate clients of commercial banks. Fully collateralized financing means that an issuer can obtain funds at a lower cost of capital. In addition, to the extent that the issuer services the underlying assets, an additional source of fee income is generated. Liquidity is much enhanced because loans and other receivables can be sold in a liquid secondary market despite the fact that the underlying assets, individually, are highly illiquid. Securitization also aids diversification in that an issuer can substitute a security backed by many loans for the same dollar cost that might be associated with only one or two individual loans. Securitization also helps to reduce interest rate risk. To the extent that there is a mismatch of the average maturity of assets versus the average maturity of liabilities, assets can be bundled and sold to alleviate the situation.

The cost of securitization may be on the order of 1 percentage point. Issuers incur investment banking fees, filing fees with the SEC and the NASD, fees to rating agencies, fees associated with the trustee or other separate entity, and private insurance, as applicable. To some extent, the cost of securitization depends on the assets in question. An investment banker should question its client about the variables that affect the cost.

- Are the credit issues relatively easy to understand and communicate?
- How easily can the cash flows of the underlying assets be estimated?
- Will the average life of the underlying assets be at least one year, ensuring an adequate return of interest payments?

- What are the historical default rates of the underlying assets?
- Do the underlying assets totally amortize?
- Are the underlying assets based on a diverse pool?
- Can the collateral of the underlying assets (for example, the homes that are collateral for mortgages) be easily liquidated, as necessary?

To the extent that the answers to these questions are favorable, the securitization is less costly. All these factors contribute to the liquidity of the issue and the size of the potential investor pool.

BASIC ELEMENTS OF
A SECURITIZATION

While the exact form of a securitization depends on the specific transaction, certain basic functions are fulfilled in each. *Originators* make the loans or create the assets that become the collateral for asset-backed securities. The entities involved in originating these assets are varied: federal agencies, commercial banks, savings and loan associations, the captive finance companies of the three major U.S. automobile manufacturers, other finance companies, computer companies, manufacturing firms, life insurance companies, and securities firms. Among the assets securitized by these originators are residential mortgage loans, automobile loans, mobile home loans, computer leases, trade receivables, and policyholder loans.

Servicers manage the underlying assets in the securitization process. These entities collect principal and interest payments, maintain records, and perform necessary collection functions. Servicers also generate monthly or annual reports with respect to the underlying assets and the value of the portfolio. Most originators or affiliates of the originators act as servicers.

The entities that actually offer the asset-backed securities are *issuers*. Usually, originators do not sell the asset-backed securities directly to investors. A bankruptcy-remote finance company is typically created. Alternative names for the issuing finance company are

- Conduit.
- Special purpose vehicle (SPV).
- Special purpose entity (SPE).
- Limited purpose corporation.

Issuers may be either subsidiaries of the originators or subsidiaries of the investment bankers. When the issuer is a subsidiary of the investment banker, it is often referred to as an *orphan subsidiary*. Issuers become bankruptcy-remote by issuing no other debt besides the asset-backed securities. Whenever additional debt is issued by the issuer, that debt is subordinated to the asset-backed securities and the claim of holders of the asset-backed securities is in no way diminished by the additional debt. In some cases, the asset-backed securities of one issuer include assets created by several originators. This situation is beneficial when individual originators have insufficient assets to create a pool that may be securitized.

Investment bankers place the asset-backed securities with investors. If the issue is a public placement, the underwriter purchases these securities and then resells them to the public. If the issue is a private placement, the investment banker acts as agent to assemble an adequate group of investors. A private placement involves less risk for the underwriter and, accordingly, a lower underwriting fee. However, a private placement is also less liquid than a public placement. As a result, the interest rate associated with privately placed asset-backed securities is higher than with a public issue. In either case, together with the issuer, the investment banker structures the issue and ensures compliance with all legal, accounting, and regulatory requirements. Note that the commitment of time and resources by an investment banker is greater, all other things being equal, for a first-time issue, an issue by an infrequent issuer, or a new type of issue.

Credit enhancers improve the credit rating and, thus, the marketability of an issue. Most asset-backed securities are credit enhanced. Credit enhancement may be provided by either the issuer or a third party. Third-party credit enhancement takes the form of a *letter of credit* or *private insurance*. The issuer can enhance an issue by establishing a senior-subordinated structure, overcollateralization, or establishing a spread account.

In a *senior-subordinated structure*, the originator assumes risk by holding the subordinated securities. *Overcollateralization* is used primarily in those structures referred to earlier as asset-backed bonds; that is, bonds that remain on the balance sheet of the originator. The objective of overcollateralization is to protect the investor from deterioration in the market value of the collateral. A *spread account* is established by the servicer. On issue, a spread account receives an advance from the servicer. After issue, any excess of cash flows beyond those necessary to make promised payments to investors and to cover servicing fees accrues to the spread account. At the time of maturity, any remaining balance in the spread account is returned to the servicer.

With respect to *financial guarantees from third parties*, a number of U.S. firms provide private insurance. In the past, most of these companies have concentrated on providing insurance for municipal bonds. Recently, they have expanded their financial guarantees to asset-backed securities. These companies are referred to as *monoline financial guarantee companies* because they are engaged in only one line of insurance business—financial guarantees.

- AMBAC Indemnity Corporation.
- Capital Guaranty Insurance Company.
- Capital Markets Assurance Company (CapMAC).
- Connie Lee Insurance Company.
- Financial Guaranty Insurance Company (FGIC).
- Financial Security Assurance, Inc. (FSA).
- Municipal Bond Investors Assurance Corporation (MBIA).

The underlying risk also may be shared with reinsurance companies.

- Asset Guaranty Reinsurance Company.
- Capital Reinsurance Company.
- Credit Reinsurance Company.
- Enhanced Reinsurance Company.

Credit Re is affiliated with Capital Re while Asset Guaranty is affiliated with Enhanced Re. Note that these companies operate throughout the United States and have recently begun to offer similar credit enhancement for asset-backed securities in Europe.

Trustees, together with issuers, establish the trusts that are part of the structure of asset-backed securities. A trust is composed of the underlying assets and has the right to receive payments due on the underlying assets. It has security interests in the collateral for the underlying assets (for example, residences that collateralize underlying mortgages), and may be a beneficiary of any insurance, including credit enhancement. A trustee is the liaison between the servicer of the asset-backed security and the investors. A trustee also acts as the contact between a credit enhancer and the investors. The Trust Indenture Act of 1939 stipulates that a bond trustee for issues in excess of $1 million must be a depository institution with a minimum capitalization of $50,000. However, Standard & Poor's, the debt rating agency, requires at least $500 million in capital. In practice, the trustees for virtually every issue of asset-backed securities that are not mortgage-related have been large money center commercial banks. The responsibilities of the trustee may be summarized as follows:

- Purchasing assets from the issuer on behalf of the trust.
- Issuing certificates to investors.
- Passing on to investors the funds the servicer deposits in the trust account.
- Reinvesting funds in the trust account if there is a time lag between date of deposit and date of payment to investors.

- Determining that reports made by the servicer to investors are adequate.
- Distributing servicer reports to investors.
- Performing the functions of the servicer if the servicer is unable to do so.

Credit rating agencies perform the same function for asset-backed securities as they do for conventional bonds.[1] In this evaluation, credit rating agencies consider the creditworthiness of the issuer (a special purpose finance company subsidiary of either the originator or the underwriter). However, the creditworthiness of the conduit is related to the underlying assets. A rating agency must evaluate how likely it is that the issuer will be able to deliver all promised payments of principal and interest. The ability to deliver promised payments, in turn, is related to all elements of the structure of the issue— underlying assets, the servicer, the trustee, and the credit enhancer.

As underwriters of asset-backed securities, commercial banks have a number of competitive advantages. The originators of the underlying assets are very often other commercial banks or other financial institutions. The vast majority of trustees are money center commercial banks. Third-party credit enhancement takes the form either of a letter of credit from a commercial bank or private insurance. For private insurance, the primary insurers are firms that also insure municipal bonds. Municipal bond underwriting is one of the areas in which commercial banks have played an active role in underwriting.

EVALUATING AND CONTROLLING CREDIT RISK

The complexity of an asset-backed security suggests that its components must be analyzed individually. Three main questions should be answered:

- What is the credit quality of the underlying assets and the entities involved in the transaction, including the originator, the servicer, the issuer, the trustee, and the credit enhancers?

- Will the cash flows from the underlying assets (including credit enhancements and liquidity supports) be sufficient to meet payment obligations to investors with respect to interest and principal?
- Is the issuer (conduit) structured in such a way that holders of the asset-backed securities have legally binding rights to the cash flows generated by the underlying assets in the event of financial distress?

An investment banker must be prepared to help a client answer these questions while structuring asset-backed securities. Because there are separate responsibilities at every level of the securitization, the functions have become quite fragmented. An investment banker must be able to evaluate each function clearly and distinctly even when two or more functions are performed by the same party. In every case, the responsibilities and contingencies associated with each function must be clearly outlined in the documentation for the transaction.

The Asset Pool

Portfolio performance of the asset pool is perhaps the most critical element of evaluating the creditworthiness of an asset-backed security. Relevant issues are projected portfolio delinquency, default rates, and the severity of loss in periods of economic distress. Asset pools generally can be classified as consumer assets, commercial assets, and focus or other assets.

Consumer assets (secured and unsecured) include retail auto loans, auto leases, credit card receivables, residential mortgage loans, and home equity loans (second mortgages). Pools of these assets, and assets like these, are typically large (250 to 500 individual loans). This creates diversification benefits in the asset pool itself. In addition, such loans often originate with homogenous credit standards and terms.

Because of these characteristics, consumer assets may be analyzed with historical statistics that provide much information about the future cash flows associated with the underlying assets. Note that studies formally correlating underwriting criteria to portfolio performance have been rare outside the residential mortgage market. Nevertheless, specific factors such as loan-to-value ratios, property types, amortization schedules, and other factors are important variables in the evaluation of an asset pool of consumer loans.

Commercial assets include equipment loans and leases, dealer inventory financing (floor plans), and trade receivables. For these, each loan is typically larger in amount. As a result, the pool may include only 50 individual credits (as compared to as many as 500 in a consumer asset pool). The larger transactions will probably be reviewed individually while smaller transactions are sampled. The results of such credit review are then weighted by the relative importance within the asset pool to assess overall creditworthiness.

Focus assets are even less standardized. These assets require a special focus on the legal and cash flow patterns not found in other assets. Examples are franchise agreements, special licensing, oil and gas rights, and mortgage servicing rights. For focus assets, specialized credit evaluation criteria must be developed that depend on the underlying assets.

Ideally, information with respect to the asset pool includes:

- Aggregate pool balance as of the cutoff date.
- Number of loans or leases.
- Average loan or lease balance.
- Weighted average yield.
- Range of interest rates.
- Weighted average remaining time to maturity.
- The range of remaining time to maturity.
- Weighted average original time to maturity.
- Range of original time to maturity.

- Weighted average loan-to-value ratio (secured assets).
- Range of loan-to-value ratios.
- New/used ratios (automobiles, boats, mobile homes, and equipment).
- Geographic distribution (state, city).
- Prepayment provisions and penalties.
- Cash flow projections.
- Fees (for example, late fees).
- Historical payments, including interest and principal.
- Historical purchase rate (especially for credit cards—rate at which balance of the underlying loans increase after securitization).
- Average credit limits.
- Delinquency status of loans.
- Concentration of obligors (individuals, industries, or other common characteristics).

Although not a complete list of pool characteristics, this does illustrate the need for all relevant information about cash flows of the asset pool. So that risk may be assessed adequately, a minimum of three years of data is required. Preferably, a five-year stream of information should be provided. Note that delinquency status and past performance of the pool have the highest correlations with asset pool performance. Thus, historical data is extremely important.

Once the pool has been analyzed, it may be necessary to *adjust the pool* to make it more attractive to investors. This internal enhancement of the pool may take one of two forms: restructuring the pool, or setting termination triggers.

Restructuring the pool means eliminating those individual assets that cause the asset pool to contain either undesirable receivables, excessive concentrations, or a higher than desired loss probability. One possible method of eliminating undesirable receivables is to remove any loans or other receivables that are overdue at the time of pool assessment. Under other circumstances, it may be desirable to eliminate assets with an original term to maturity over a specified maximum. Such selection filters depend on the nature of the asset pool and the perceived preferences of investors. Eliminating excessive concentrations may center around specific industries, geographic regions, or other variables that would suggest an unacceptable reduction of diversification. Examples might include eliminating any assets that represent more than a 10 percent concentration within a particular industry. Again, the specific filter depends on the portfolio and perceived investor preferences.

The objective of restructuring the pool is to reduce maximum anticipated loss to an acceptable level. To achieve this, it is necessary to associate a probability of loss with each individual asset in the pool. By multiplying this probability (or anticipated loss proportion) by the face amount of the asset, a dollar amount of anticipated loss can be generated. When the results of this calculation are summed across all assets in the asset pool, the expected loss of the entire portfolio may be estimated.

$$EL = \sum_{i=1}^{N} p_i A_i \qquad (1)$$

where

EL = Expected loss
p_i = Loss proportion of asset i
A_i = Face amount of asset i
N = Total amount of individual assets

Clearly, calculating expected loss is not a precise science because it requires a subjective assessment of future loss. However, it does serve an important function in that it focuses on expectations in connection with each of the assets of the pool. This permits subsequent monitoring of the asset pool to be framed by variance from expectations.

If the asset pool consists of receivables calling for regular asset substitutions, the integrity of the entire pool can be protected by instituting *termination triggers*. This situation may occur when short-term assets are being used as collateral for the asset-backed security. Examples of such short-term arrangements may be credit card receivables or trade receivables. A termination trigger prevents deterioration in the asset portfolio of the originator from contaminating the asset pool of the asset-backed security. Suppose, for example, that the historical default rate on the originator's loan portfolio is 1 percent per year. The termination trigger may require that no further assets be transferred into the trust if the originator's default experience increases to 2 percent per year. In this case, the asset-backed security would accept no further assets from the originator.

Should the same factors that impacted the originator's loan portfolio begin to impact assets held in trust for the asset-backed security, prearranged credit enhancements would protect investors. That is, excessive default losses would be absorbed by the credit enhancer rather than the investors in the asset-backed security.

The Originator

The credit risk associated with the *originator* falls into several categories:

- The legal risk associated with asset transfers.
- The potential effect of the originator's bankruptcy on the quality of the assets in the pool.
- The necessary credit support to protect investors.

The originator generally transfers assets to the asset pool through a *true sale* or a *transfer of title*. This process involves amending certificates of title and/or filing UCC–1 financing statements.[2] If these documents are not filed, in the event of bankruptcy, investors may not be permitted to benefit from the sale of collateral for the underlying loans and receivables. Also, in the event of bankruptcy, a credit card asset pool may be prohibited from receiving additional individual assets as stipulated in the indenture for the asset-backed security. Note that this is less of a problem with financial institutions than with retail operations. For example, if a savings and loan association becomes insolvent, the credit card portfolio may be absorbed by a stronger financial institution that takes over the failed thrift. On the other hand, a retail operation may be unwound with no new receivables generated.

An *originator's bankruptcy* also can impact an asset-backed security in ways not directly related to credit. When individual assets are collateralized by vehicles or other equipment, the quality of service for the collateral is impacted if the originator becomes insolvent. If the manufacturer of the collateral has financial difficulties, this may impact the quality of the collateral itself, prompting transaction disputes and product returns. In turn, nonpayment on individual pool assets results. Such nonpayment circumstances are referred to as dilution of trade receivables or retail credit card receivables.

Both effective ownership of pool assets and potential for dilution have an impact on the appropriate level of *credit enhancement*. Specific provisions for credit enhancement may be necessary to compensate for a dispute with respect to titles of individual assets in the asset pool and dilution of the receivables.

As a result of these considerations, the credit of the originator is a crucial element in the evaluation of a potential asset-backed security. The areas that should be examined are

- Sourcing of credit or loan applications.
- Credit review of applications.
- Appraisals of collateral (as applicable).
- Credit approval guidelines.
- Documentation of loans.
- Disbursement procedures.
- Overall portfolio performance.
- Representations and warranties of the originator as compared to actual portfolio performance.

Exhibit 5–2 contains the credit ratings that may be given to an originator by Standard & Poor's. These ratings range from Strong to Weak. A rating of Strong can be earned by an originator with a management team competent in underwriting practices. The rating agency also expects that conservative standards have been set with respect to generating individual assets. There is an implicit expectation that the originator has made an adequate investment in technology so that in-house information

E X H I B I T 5–2

Credit Rating of the Originator of an Asset-Backed Security

S&P Rating	Characteristics of Originator
Strong	Highest ranking: Strong and stable management, highly effective production capacity, use of conservative underwriting standards to generate individual loans or receivables, quality control systems that exceed industry standards, superior loan servicing operations
Above average	Differs from highest ranking only by a small margin: Differences relate to track record, stability, flexibility, or financial condition
Average	Variable track record: Variability may relate to nontraditional underwriting standards to generate individual loans or receivables, delinquencies near the national average, loan servicing adequate but not incorporating the most recent industry innovations, overall improving performance
Below average	Lack of ability, productivity, and competence: Variable track record, underwriting consistently more liberal than traditional standards, marginal loan servicing capability, overall declining performance
Weak	Poor track record: Underwriting exclusively more liberal than traditional standards, inadequate quality control, recurring losses, servicing capability overextended, delinquencies far exceed national averages

Source: Clifford M. Griep, "Structured Securities: Credit, Cash Flow, and Legal Risks," in *The Global Asset-Backed Securities Market: Structuring, Managing and Allocating Risk* (Chicago: Probus Publishing Company, 1993), pp. 140–41.

management is more than adequate for the assets in the pool and ongoing operations. Ability to service assets is important because many originators are also servicers.

At the other extreme, a Weak rating indicates firms have used underwriting standards much more liberal than industry standards would suggest. A firm also might receive this rating when quality control is poor and the technology and human capital necessary to adequately service loans is inadequate. A firm with a Weak rating will have experienced losses in its underwriting activities, often associated with high levels of delinquencies.

All of the preceding is not to suggest that it is merely the creditworthiness of the originator that determines the viability of the issue. However, serious problems with respect to the originator can doom a securitization to failure.

The Servicer

Most asset-backed securities transactions have direct credit exposure in connection with the *servicer*. This exposure arises because the servicer holds funds that will be distributed to investors. To the extent that servicers pass along payments from pool assets to the trustee on a daily basis, this exposure is minimized. However, some asset-backed securities are structured so payments from the servicer to investors are at intervals that are less frequent than the receipt of payments from pool assets. For example, in some credit card asset-backed securities, the servicer may commingle funds for up to 70 days. Here the exposure to servicer credit risk is relatively high.

According to the terms of the indenture, a servicer may provide a cash advance covering delinquencies that may be ultimately recoverable. This cash advance process protects investors from uneven cash flows, that is, liquidity risk. The credit of the servicer is directly linked to the creditworthiness of the asset-backed security. In evaluating the servicer, a number of variables are considered. Some of these variables are similar to those scrutinized in an examination of the originator. Recall that sometimes the originator may continue to act as the servicer in a particular transaction. Nevertheless, the two functions are distinct and must be evaluated as such.

In the area of collections, a servicer must demonstrate the ability to meet servicing needs by having adequate staff and systems. The important functions of the servicer are timing and prioritization of collection actions, policies and practices that involve rewriting or restructuring individual assets, terms relating to the extension of due dates, and forbearance policies (declining to exercise a legal right against a borrower in default). Another important element of the responsibilities of a servicer are procedures with respect to recoveries. Collecting amounts associated with previously defaulted individual assets benefits investors either directly or indirectly because such cash proceeds help reimburse the expenses of collection activities.

Depending on the nature of the assets in the pool, servicers may have considerable discretion in managing the assets. For example, transactions that involve multifamily and commercial mortgages typically give servicers considerable discretion in loan restructuring, foreclosures, and other collection activities. In such a case, a transaction should be structured periodically to review practices and procedures adopted and followed by the servicer.

The servicer should be evaluated along several basic criteria:

- Servicing history.
- Servicing experience.
- Servicing capabilities.
- Origination policies and procedures (as applicable).
- Management competence.
- Adequacy of staff.
- Potential for growth in the servicing industry.
- Degree of competition from other servicers.
- Overall business environment.
- Financial condition of servicer.

Note that the financial condition of servicers can vary significantly. Some servicers are subsidiaries of originating entities, with adequate capital and capital reserves (in the form of parent company capitalization). Other servicers are stand-alone operations with limited working capital. In the latter case, a servicer is less able to add staff for either processing or collections when circumstances warrant. All servicers should be able to demonstrate the ability to fulfill necessary functions throughout the life of the asset-backed security.

If a servicer may not be able to fulfill its responsibilities under the terms of the transactions, provisions should be made for the substitution of servicers. Alternatively, a larger, better capitalized organization can be specified as a master servicer to which the responsibility would fall in the event of default on the part of the original servicer.

The Issuer

The underlying issuer (or conduit or special purpose vehicle) must be structured to protect both the asset pool and the claims of the investors. If the originator in the transaction is eligible to seek protection under bankruptcy laws, such protection will prohibit anyone from taking action against the property of the originator. If the individual assets in the asset pool are deemed to be property of the originator, then the collateral for the asset-backed security is jeopardized. Also, some bankruptcy procedures require a secured creditor to exchange the original collateral for another form of collateral. For example, a lien on liquid assets, such as receivables, may be replaced by a lien on plant and equipment. Such a substitution significantly alters the cash flows generated by the asset pool. This alteration would cause the asset-backed security to default. Even if receivables are exchanged for receivables, the credit quality of the asset pool could be materially affected by the substitution, again exposing investors to credit risk.

For these reasons, the issuer must be structured in a way that creates a bankruptcy-remote entity, either in the

form of a trust, corporation, or partnership. The characteristics that cause the issuer to be bankruptcy-remote will be
contained in the entity's bylaws. In addition, these provisions also should be included in the documentation for the
asset-backed securities so that investors fully appreciate
protections that may exist. Specifically, the issuer must:

- Limit its activities to the asset-backed securities
  transaction in question.
- Engage in no other business.
- Be prohibited from incurring any debt other than
  that associated with the asset-backed security issue.
  The only acceptable exception to debt issuance is
  the issuance of debt fully subordinated to the asset-
  backed security, nonrecourse in nature, payable only
  from excess cash, and not constituting a claim
  enforceable against the issuer in a bankruptcy proceeding.
- Be prohibited from merging or consolidating with
  any other entity, unless the surviving entity is also
  bankruptcy-remote.

Issuers are very often subsidiaries of originators.[3] In
the event of the originator's bankruptcy, it is critical that
the issuer not be consolidated with the parent in the bankruptcy proceeding. When consolidation occurs, the issue of
substitution of collateral and other problematic situations
jeopardize the security of investors. In deciding whether a
consolidation is reasonable, courts generally consider factors such as the degree of difficulty in segregating the
assets and liabilities of the two entities, the presence or
absence of consolidated financial statements, commingling
of assets and business functions, and the extent to which
ownership and other interest is shared between the issuer
(subsidiary) and the originator (parent). To perfect a separation of the originator and the issuer, the following should
be considered:

- Separate officers and directors.
- Separate books and records.

- Periodic and regular meetings of the board of directors of the issuer.
- Separate offices.
- Separate bank accounts.
- Payment of issuer's expenses by the issuer (not by the originator).
- No benefit to issuer from intercompany guarantees.
- Statement and warranty by the originator that it is not responsible for debts of the issuer.

Another key area in maintaining the bankruptcy-remote status for the issuer is the integrity of the transfer of title of individual assets in the asset pool. The transfer must be a true sale. This status is not necessarily guaranteed simply because of a purchase and sale agreement between the issuer and the originator. Sometimes courts may decide that the transfer of the assets to the issuer was a collateralized borrowing on the part of the parent. Then the assets would be considered part of the property of the originator and subject to bankruptcy proceedings for the originator. The following questions can assist in establishing an issuer so this circumstance becomes less likely.

- Does the issuer have the right of recourse to other assets of the originator if the individual assets in the asset pool do not provide sufficient cash flow?
- Do the issuer's rights in the property end if the receivables or loans are paid with funds from another source?
- Must the issuer account to the originator for any cash flows received from the pool assets if these amounts exceed the amount of the obligation at the time that the pool is formed and transferred?
- Does the language in the purchase and sale document indicate an intention to make an assignment rather than a sale?
- Does the sale discharge an obligation of the originator?

Because these are highly technical issues, an investment banker is well advised to seek a legal opinion establishing an effective legal transfer of assets. The ability to demonstrate protection from consolidation with the originator and a failed legal transfer of assets is directly related to the protection of investors and the ability to establish a credit rating based on the assets in the pool.

The Trustee

Like the servicer, the *trustee* must demonstrate the ability to perform its responsibilities over the term of the asset-backed security. The responsibilities of the trustee include management of trust funds and accounts, tracking payment streams on a monthly or quarterly basis, reporting to investors and other concerned entities on a monthly or quarterly basis, and the ability to act as a servicer in the event that the originally designated servicer fails to fulfill its responsibilities.

While the trustee has less direct contact with the pool assets or the cash flows from the assets, the inability of the trustee to perform its duties may delay payments. The confidence in the trustee to fulfill these duties can perhaps best be established by assigning a trustee that has an investment grade credit rating.[4] Another provision in the documentation for the asset-backed security that adds confidence in the structure is provision for a substitute trustee in the event that the original trustee is unable to perform its functions. Of course, the experience of a trustee in handling such issues is also an important element in the evaluation of trustee credit risk.

Credit Enhancement

Credit enhancement can be provided for the issue either through external means or by specific internal structures. Bank letters of credit and private insurance are the most common external means of credit enhancement. The general rule is that the credit enhancer should have a credit rating no lower than the credit rating of the asset-backed security without credit enhancement. This theory of the weakest link suggests that the credit is only as strong as the credit of the weakest participant in the structure.

Many times external credit support is not provided for the entire amount of the asset pool, but only for the anticipated loss or maximum tolerable loss of the asset pool. If the asset pool is amortizing, as is true with mortgage loans, the credit enhancement may step down as the unpaid balance of the assets pool declines. Some transactions with step-down provisions permit the step-down only in the event that the actual loss experience, perhaps during the first five years, is within predetermined limits.

Internal methods of credit enhancement include (1) cash collateral or reserve accounts and (2) senior-subordinated structures. *Reserve accounts* are established in some cases in lieu of letters of credit. Then, a commercial bank typically lends funds to the issuer on behalf of the investors and the cash is held in liquid, investment-grade instruments available to cover portfolio delinquencies and losses. The types of investments appropriate for these funds are

- U.S. government obligations, obligations guaranteed by the U.S. government, or federal agency securities.
- Demand deposits, time deposits, or certificates of deposit from a U.S. national bank, state-chartered bank, or other equivalent depository institution with a high investment grade.
- Bankers' acceptances from similarly rated institutions.
- Commercial paper with top credit ratings.
- Money market funds with top credit ratings, specifically those that invest in the instruments indicated earlier.

The *senior-subordinated structure* is an example of the way pay-through bonds provide credit protection for certain tranches. Four basic types of senior-subordinated structures provide credit protection for the senior instruments—fast pay/slow pay, shifting interest, fixed amount, and step-down mechanisms.

Fast pay/slow pay is a structure in which 100 percent of all principal collections, including prepayments, is paid to the senior class investors. In this structure, the payback to the senior certificate holders is accelerated, shortening the length of time that the certificate holder is exposed to credit and other risks.

In a *shifting interest* transaction, some payments can be allocated to the subordinated tranche(s) earlier than they would otherwise be allocated. In this situation, however, the senior certificate holders must receive all cash flows to which they are entitled before the subordinated certificate holders receive any cash distribution. To the extent that subordinated certificate holders receive payments, the degree of internal credit support is reduced.

An alternative structure is the *fixed amount* arrangement. The subordinated certificates are obligated to absorb a specified percentage of the senior investors' exposure to loss. Beyond this specified amount, the subordinated certificate holders are not obligated to absorb losses that may occur.

As noted previously, for external credit support the internal *step-down* mechanism is appropriate for amortizing assets, such as mortgage loans, home equity loans, and manufactured housing loans. For example, a subordinated class of certificates may absorb all the losses incurred by a senior class of certificates until certain thresholds are reached. Consider a structure in which the senior certificates represent 85 percent of the original amount of the asset pool, with subordinated certificates representing the balance. A declining subordination may require that the subordinated certificates absorb losses sustained by the senior class until the senior class is amortized down to 70 percent of the unpaid mortgage balance. At this point, the two classes of certificates absorb losses based on some other formula, perhaps in proportional shares.

Credit enhancements are varied and continue to evolve as the structure of asset-backed securities continues to evolve. The best structures include a combination of both external and internal credit support.

MORTGAGE-BACKED PASS-THROUGH SECURITIES

Beginning in 1970, the Government National Mortgage Association (GNMA or Ginnie Mae) stimulated the secondary market in mortgage loans by creating a pass-through vehicle that issued *participation certificates*, backed by pools of residential mortgage loans. This innovation made it possible for mortgage originators to move mortgages off their balance sheets and generate an on-going source of funding, while retaining servicing rights. These participation certificates represented proportional claims on the pool of mortgage loan assets. Other pass-through vehicles have been created by the Federal Home Loan Mortgage Corporation (FHLMC) and the Federal National Mortgage Association (FNMA). Within the private sector, commercial banks have been particularly active in this securitization process. The total servicing fee is generally around 50 basis points, including approximately 6 basis points for agency guarantees of principal and interest, as applicable.

GNMA pass-through securities are backed only by FHA/VA loans, while FNMA and FHLMC obligations are backed primarily by conventional mortgage loans. GNMA pass-through certificates are issued through a trust, while FNMA and FHLMC certificates create their own structures. GNMA loans are of only one type and of recent origination with similar interest rates and maturity. FNMA and FHLMC certificates, on the other hand, may be backed by more seasoned loans with varying interest rates and maturity dates. GNMA and FNMA guarantee the timely payment of both principal and interest, while FHLMC guarantees the timely payment of interest and the ultimate payment of principal. In terms of volume, GNMA pass-through certificates represent the most active market.

Aside from default risk, however, investors in mortgage-backed pass-through securities face *reinvestment risk* and *prepayment risk*. Because mortgage loans are amortizing assets, investors receive return of principal and interest with each payment. Unlike a conventional bond, in which principal repayment is at the end of a term of the bond, a pass-through security returns the bulk of invested principal well before maturity. Hence, reinvestment risk is significantly higher. Prepayment risk may be considerable, depending on economic conditions. Prepayments occur for a number of reasons—sale of a home, unexpected availability of funds to repay a mortgage, refinancing a mortgage, or lifestyle changes (such as retirement or divorce).

In addition to fixed-rate loans, pass-through securities have been issued against adjustable-rate mortgages (ARMs). FHLMC issued pass-throughs collateralized by ARMs with rates tied to Treasury rates, including a 2 percent annual cap and a 6 percent lifetime cap. FNMA has issued similar securities. In addition, FHLMC has introduced mortgage-backed pass-through securities backed by ARMs that carry the option to convert to fixed-rate loans.

Prepayment assumptions are critical in the evaluation of the asset pool for mortgage-backed securities. There are essentially five methods of estimating prepayment rates:

1. Twelve-year prepaid life.
2. Constant prepayment rate (CPR).
3. FHA experience.
4. Public Securities Association (PSA) model.
5. Econometric prepayment models.

The *12-year prepaid life* method assumes no prepayments for the first 12 years of a pass-through's life and that full prepayment will be at the end of the 12th year. This approach is based on FHA data that showed the average mortgage terminated in the 12th year. Clearly this is a false assumption. Prepayment rates fluctuate depending on the general level of interest rates and specific mortgage characteristics. Also, mortgages with high interest rates prepay faster than those with low interest rates. This method is rarely used now.

The *CPR* is the percentage of mortgages outstanding at the beginning of a period that will terminate during that period. The CPR is expressed as an annual rate, while monthly prepayment rates are usually referred to as single monthly mortality (SMM) or constant monthly prepayment (CMP). In constructing an amortization schedule, the SMM is applied to the unpaid balance of a mortgage after the normal, scheduled principal payment is made.

FHA experience projects a prepayment rate of the asset pool relative to the historical prepayment and default experience of FHA-insured, 30-year mortgage loans. Periodically, FHA publishes a table of 30 statistics that represent the survivorship of FHA-insured mortgages. For a specific pool of mortgages, the prepayment assumption is expressed as some percentage of FHA experience. For example, a pool expected to mimic the performance of FHA mortgages has a 100 percent FHA prepayment assumption associated with it. If the pool is expected to prepay at twice the rate, the prepayment rate assumption will be 200 percent FHA experience. Currently, this approach is not widely used.

The *PSA* model is currently the industry standard. This approach combines FHA survivorship schedules with the CPR approach. Essentially the assumption is that prepayments are relatively low in the first 30 months, although increasing. After the 30th month, the rate of prepayment stabilizes. Specifically, the PSA benchmark (100 percent PSA) assumes that the first month prepayment will be 0.2 percent, the second month 0.4 percent, the third month 0.6 percent, and so on. This continues until the 30th month after mortgage origination. At this time, the CPR is 6 percent and remains so until the mortgage pool is completely amortized. If the assumption is that prepayments are twice as high as PSA, then these percentages are doubled (200 percent PSA). If the assumption is that the prepayment rates are half this rate, the percentages are halved (50 percent PSA).

Investment banks have developed proprietary *econometric prepayment models*. In essence, SMMs are projected for each remaining month of the mortgage pool. This vector of SMMs reflects variation in season and age of the underlying individual assets, as well as changing patterns of housing sales and refinancings. While more involved, such models may be preferable to CPR or PSA rates that do not consider changing economic factors.

The mortgage-backed pass-through market is dominated by the federal agencies noted earlier. Although private firms have issued relatively few such securities, there are a few examples. Bank of America issued the first private-sector pass-through in 1977. These securities were backed by conventional mortgages and credit-enhanced by private insurance that covered the entire pool of assets. Generally, the activity in this market by private sector firms has been limited, with many more issuing securities in the pay-through market.

MORTGAGE-BACKED PAY-THROUGH BONDS

The category of mortgage-backed pay-through bonds is perhaps best represented by the classification *collateralized mortgage obligations* (CMOs). In 1983, FHLMC issued the first CMO. These early pay-through bonds were divided into three maturity classes, with each receiving semiannual interest payments. Class 1 bondholders received principal payments and all prepayments until this tranche was completely paid off. At that time, Class 2 bondholders received principal payments and prepayments until completely amortized. At that time, Class 3 began to receive principal payments. The first FHLMC CMO was structured so that Class 1 bonds were repaid in 5 years from issue date, Class 2 bonds within 12 years, and Class 3 bonds within 20 years.

The newer variations of the CMO include a Z-bond or accrual bond and a residual class. After the three classes are repaid, the Z-bond receives regular interest and principal payments along with interest accrued during the period that Classes 1, 2, and 3 were being amortized. The residual class receives all payments in excess of those devoted to Classes 1, 2, and 3 and the Z-bond.

While FHLMC initiated the CMO market, the majority of issues in this market have private sector issuers. Banks and thrifts use the residual class to hedge their mortgage portfolios. When interest rates rise, the market value of existing low-rate mortgages falls and prepayment rates are low. During these periods, the residual class of CMOs realizes higher income because the rate of prepayment is lower than assumed in the original pricing of the CMO and the residual receives the unanticipated interest payments.

The residual class also can receive payments as a result of differences between reinvestment assumptions and actual reinvestment opportunities. If the trustee assumes a conservative reinvestment rate, any additional interest earned as a result of higher interest rates accrues to the residual class.

From the perspective of the investment bankers, CMOs can be a significant source of revenue. Investors can purchase specific securities with fairly predictable repayment patterns, effectively avoiding the issue of prepayment risk. As a result, investors are willing to pay a higher price for the securities. To the extent that the investment banker is able to sell the pay-through bonds for a higher price than the underlying mortgages, this difference accrues to the investment banker. Investment bankers also can tap into this market by aggregating the loans of a number of originators and renting an existing issuer through which mortgages can be sold and economies of scale realized.

Since the generic CMOs were introduced, several *derivative mortgage products* have been developed. Generally, these may be classified as planned amortization classes (PACs), targeted amortization classes (TACs), interest only (IOs) and principal-only (POs) securities, and floating-rate CMOs.

Planned amortization classes (PACs) guarantee investors a rate of amortization similar to a sinking fund amortization on a conventional bond. In essence, PACs guarantee that the pay down schedule remains the same as long as prepayments remain in a given, specified range. This range is called the *prepayment band*. Clearly, the PAC reduces even more uncertainty than is normal for a CMO tranche. However, the uncertainty that is removed for the PAC tranche is transferred to another class of security. The class of security that absorbs prepayment risk for the PACs is *companion bonds*. Because PACs are relatively free of prepayment risk, PAC bondholders accept a lower interest rate. Because companion bonds absorb this prepayment risk, companion bondholders expect a higher interest rate.

Targeted amortization classes (TACs) are scheduled to receive a specified monthly principal repayment. Any excess principal repayment is distributed to non-TAC classes. If principal repayments are less than the amount necessary to provide TAC classes with the scheduled principal repayment, the shortfall lengthens the TAC tranche's life.

Interest-only and *principal-only* tranches are created when payments are separated into these two components. When interest rates decline, mortgages are more frequently prepaid, and PO investors receive their return more quickly than usual. This early payment of principal benefits PO investors. On the other hand, rapid prepayment shortens the stream of interest payments to IO investors, to their disadvantage. When interest rates increase, the reverse effect is realized. PO tranches appeal to investors who anticipate interest rate declines, while IO tranches appeal to investors who believe interest rates will increase.

Because the tranches of CMOs are so varied in their financial structure, they must be evaluated individually. Recently, Fitch Investors Service has developed a measure of volatility for CMO tranches. These so-called V-ratings attempt to analyze the potential impact of interest rate movements on individual tranches but do not attempt to anticipate the probability of specific interest rate scenarios. The following information is used in the V-ratings:

- Indications of volatility by individual measures of total return, price, and duration.
- Identification of significant contributing factors to individual tranche volatility, including high or low

coupons and individual tranche prepayment collars (combination of interest-rate caps and floors).

- Indication of the interest rate environments in which individual tranches show greatest positive and negative performance potential.

The five ratings are defined as follows:

1. **V1**—Exhibits relatively small changes in total value, total return, and cash flow in all interest rate scenarios used in the model.

2. **V2**—Exhibits relatively small changes in total value, total return, and cash flow in most modeled interest rate scenarios. Under certain adverse interest rate scenarios, one or more of the indicators are more volatile than V1.

3. **V3**—Exhibits relatively larger changes in total return, total value, and cash flow in all model interest rate scenarios. However, cash flow indicators are less volatile than federal agency certificates.

4. **V4**—Exhibits greater changes in total return, price, and cash flow than current federal agency certificates in all modeled interest rate scenarios.

5. **V5**—Exhibits substantial changes in total return, price, and cash flow in all modeled interest rate scenarios compared to federal agency certificates. Under the most stressful interest rate scenarios, negative total returns may result.

While these V-ratings are not specific, they are at least the beginning of a rating scheme for these complex, often poorly understood instruments. This information management is critical in the further development of asset-backed securities as the industry continues to evolve.

THE DIRECTION OF THE INDUSTRY

As entrants in the investment banking field, commercial banks are well prepared to enter and participate in the asset-backed securities market. The challenge is not so much identifying adequately collateralized and underwritten individual assets in an asset pool. Instead, the challenge is to manage the composition of the securitized pool and to communicate fairly and adequately the risks and rewards associated with each class of the security.

SELECTED REFERENCES

Carlson, John H., and Frank J. Fabozzi, eds. *The Trading and Securitization of Senior Bank Loans.* Chicago: Probus Publishing Company, 1992.

Fabozzi, Frank J., and T. Dessa Fabozzi, eds. *Current Topics in Investment Management.* New York: Harper & Row, Ballinger Division, 1990.

Pavel, Christine A. *Securitization: The Analysis and Development of the Loan-Based/Asset-Backed Securities Markets.* Chicago: Probus Publishing Company, 1989.

Stone, Charles; Anne Zissu; and Jess Lederman, eds. *The Global Asset-Backed Securities Market: Structuring, Managing and Allocating Risk.* Chicago: Probus Publishing Company, 1993.

ENDNOTES

1. See Chapter 4 for a discussion of bond ratings.

2. UCC is an acronym for the Uniform Commercial Code, a set of standardized state laws that govern financial contracts. Contracts covered by the UCC include negotiable instruments (checks, drafts, and other negotiable instruments), bank deposits, letters of credit, warehouse receipts, other documents of title, and secured loans.

3. The other possibility is that the issuer would be a subsidiary of the investment banker, in which case it is referred to as an orphan subsidiary.

4. Recall that the trustee is typically a bank with capital in excess of $500 million.

CHAPTER 6

Future Trends in Commercial and Investment Banking

INTRODUCTION

All analysts of the commercial banking industry agree that increased fee income and other revenues will be essential for the future viability of the industry. Investment banking activities are part of an increasingly wider array of services offered by commercial banks. In the future, as Glass-Steagall barriers continue to erode, or are completely dismantled, expansion of these activities is inevitable. A major attraction of investment banking is that it can be a profitable addition to traditional commercial banking services.

However, investment banking is a cyclical business. As such, it contributes to a portfolio of lines of business for an institution. Understanding the cyclicality of investment banking requires a different management perspective than the more uniform profitability of commercial banks.

Understanding the different culture in the investment banking arena is also a challenge. In the future, these cultures will blend.

The demand for financing in capital markets will intensify in the future. Corporate issuers prefer flexibility in financing outside of traditional bank lending and increasingly will be able to obtain it. Internationally, enterprises that have been operated by governments will continue to be privatized, requiring large amounts of capital for securities investments. As pension funds grow in developed and developing countries, increasing capital will become available. At the same time, margins in traditional commercial banking will continue to face pressure from competition and this pressure will encourage commercial bankers to enter the securities arena.

In the future, investment bankers will be involved in more private placements of debt and equity. Both public and private placements will increasingly occur across national boundaries. U.S. commercial banks will be affected by these trends. Each institution must decide what role it will play in this new environment. Not to do so implies that the institution will relegate itself to a passive position of allowing the bank's competition to decide its fate.

PROFITS AND INVESTMENT BANKING

Internationally, commercial banks are fighting for business in loan syndications. The problem for banks is excess capital that has been built up as a result of past write-offs and regulatory direction. Commercial banks are now overprovided and extremely well capitalized. At the same time, nonfinancial corporations have improved in their own credit quality and actively have been taking advantage of equity and bond markets. Essentially, bank capital is chasing a stable or declining pool of top-tier borrowers. In addition, many of those corporates that are borrowing are refinancing old bank loans at lower interest rates. In addition, in an international context, borrowings are being extended for longer terms for banks' top-tier clients. In the United States, some borrowings that were once one-year deals are now three- to five-year arrangements. In Europe, the term of five to seven years is increasingly common.

Another trend in loan syndication internationally is a relaxation of the terms of loan documentation. Restrictive covenants are becoming increasingly more lenient. For their part, corporate customers are becoming more sophisticated in their relationships with commercial banks. Many recognize that the best way to obtain aggressive terms on loans is to link the lending business to other business. This is a reaffirmation of the concept of relationship banking. The most successful commercial banks will recognize this trend and capitalize on it by having investment banking facilities available to their clients.

However, investment banking profits can be volatile. In the United States, as long-term interest rates declined in the early 1990s, companies actively refinanced debt. New issuances of lower-cost bonds boosted the fee income associated with underwriting activity. In addition, investors became more interested in high-yielding bonds and in equities because the average rate paid by a money-market mutual fund fell below 3 percent in 1993, as compared to 9 percent at the beginning of the decade. The commissions associated with investor purchases of stocks and bonds also added to investment banking firms' profits attributable to secondary market trading.

However, beginning in February 1994, interest rate increases by the Federal Reserve drastically reduced both the inclination of corporations to enter or refinance in bond markets and investors' appetites for securities. Reduced enthusiasm for securities was particularly evident in the bond market, where bond mutual funds experienced a net outflow of approximately $40 billion in 1994, as compared to a net inflow of $25 billion in the previous year. This activity severely dampened prices in the bond markets. Adding to problems associated with high interest rates was a depressed market for mortgage-backed securities. Higher interest rates meant that homeowners were less inclined to refinance their existing mortgages. This sharply increased the period of time over which investors in mortgage-backed securities received repayment of their investment. As a result, prices fell and liquidity in the market evaporated.

Even attempts by investment banks to hedge their own portfolios used in proprietary trading proved unsuccessful.

Hedging strategies were inadequate to compensate for such abrupt, sharp rises in interest rates. Among the U.S. bulge bracket firms, the effect was devastating.[1] The profits of Merrill Lynch, Salomon Brothers, Morgan Stanley, Lehman Brothers, and Bear Stearns fell from an aggregate of $3.7 billion in 1993 to approximately $2 billion in 1994. Investors recognized the inherent volatility of investment bank earnings attributable both to underwriting and proprietary trading and reduced the premium paid for stocks in investment banking firms. Earlier in the 1990s, investment bank stocks frequently traded for two times book value. Currently, a 20 to 30 percent premium over book value is more likely.

At the same time, the investment banking industry has learned valuable lessons from the experience immediately following the stock market crash in 1987. Most investment banking firms have aggressively cut costs since that time and resisted urges to expand aggressively during the early 1990s.

Nevertheless, there is overcapacity in the industry. As is true in commercial banking, often too many investment bankers are chasing too few deals. This has led to a reduction in underwriting fees from an average of 2.2 percent of the value of the deal in 1993 to just over 1 percent currently.

The clear alternative for investment banking is to increase the size of the market. In this respect, investment bankers and commercial bankers will compete. The lines of business that show the greatest promise for market expansion are mergers and acquisitions, privatizations of previously state-owned enterprises, and retail-based securities. In the United States, consolidation in the healthcare, defense, and telecommunications industries have provided increased opportunities for securities underwriting. Privatizations in other countries have led to a significantly heightened demand for U.S. investment banking services. Having the capacity to reach a larger retail base of clients, perhaps through the offering of proprietary mutual funds, enables investment bankers to increase their placing capacity. Another area in which investment banks may stabilize their earnings is merchant banking.[2] Taking a position in a client company through merchant banking enables an institution to sell those investments at whatever point the market suggests is advantageous to do so. Of course, market conditions can move against the institution before investments are sold. Nevertheless, merchant banking does help diversify the financial transactions of investment banks.

THE CASE OF GOLDMAN SACHS

Goldman Sachs is one of the most respected and well established investment banking firms in the United States. The firm's recent difficulties illustrate certain important principles for the future of investment banking and the role of commercial banks in the industry. The successful investment banking firm of the future will have a strong sense of internal controls, diversified risk, efficiency standards, and client relationships.

Goldman Sachs has had a long-standing collegial culture and is Wall Street's only remaining private partnership. Because of the effect of rising interest rates in 1994 and ill-fated overseas activities, profits for the venerable firm plunged to $508 million in 1994 as compared to $2.3 billion in 1993. This earnings decline occurred despite healthy returns in mergers and acquisitions, equity underwriting (including initial public offerings), and international underwriting transactions. These results also fly in the face of the firm's reputation as a well-managed investment bank with strong human capital, market sophistication, and financial resources. Goldman Sachs is now undergoing a complete reengineering; it is examining all issues including compensation, planning, proprietary trading, expenses, and risk management. Even the private partnership structure is being evaluated.

These concerns follow a period of rapid expansion within Goldman Sachs. In many cases, this expansion was associated with a different shift in business focus. The firm began operations shortly after the Civil War in the United

States. Marcus Goldman was a Bavarian immigrant who visited businesses in downtown Manhattan and bought the promissory notes of their customers. At the time, bank credit was extremely difficult to obtain. Goldman Sachs filled a real need for finance for many companies. This emphasis on commercial paper was maintained until well after World War I.

As its relationship with large and growing American firms became firmly established, Goldman Sachs began to sell its clients' equity. Many companies began to rely heavily on Goldman Sachs for financing. During the 1980s, Goldman Sachs helped companies defend against hostile takeovers. The company had gained the reputation of being a tough negotiator that defended its client first and foremost. Its conservatism was evidenced by the relatively slow pace at which it entered commodities trading, asset management, the swap market, and international expansion.

In 1990, John Weinberg retired as chairman of Goldman Sachs. At this time, Robert Rubin (now U.S. Secretary of the Treasury) and Stephen Friedman became cochairmen of Goldman Sachs. The firm began to move in a decidedly more aggressive direction. Proprietary trading and international expansion received much higher priority. The management style of the firm was set by a group of comparatively young and aggressive partners. [Goldman partners are expected to retire and make way for younger partners before the age of 50 in most cases. On retirement, general partners become limited partners.]

Soon after this change in the top position, Goldman Sachs established the Water Street Fund to invest its own capital in distressed securities. However, as the firm gained control through senior debt positions, restructurings often were forced on the company involved. In these restructurings, equity holders and subordinated debt holders were often left with worthless securities. This hawkish position was a sharp departure from the previous position of Goldman as defender of firms. To further compound the effect, many of the investors who found their securities rendered worthless were Goldman Sachs clients. In 1991, the fund was liquidated and the managing partners of the fund left the firm. Recently, the Whitehall Street Real Estate LP Fund has taken positions in distressed real estate. In one case, the fund forced Cadillac Fairview, a major Canadian real estate developer, into Canadian bankruptcy court. Again, Goldman Sachs is seen as having forced investors into difficult positions. Some of these investors are clients of Goldman Sachs.

Internationally, Goldman Sachs has been no less aggressive. In 1994, Goldman Sachs increased its Hong Kong staff to almost 500. The firm has been so bullish on China that it has invested $100 million of its own capital in power plants and real estate projects. The hard-driving tactics of the Goldman staff has caused at least one Chinese deal to fall through because of what was perceived as excessive demands for returns to investors. In one case, the firm expected a 20 percent rate of return for investors in a Shandong power plant. When the State Council in the People's Republic of China objected, the privatization was canceled. Goldman Sachs also has found that underwriting spreads have been thinner than expected in its Asian operations. In the privatization of Singapore Telecom, the firm's underwriting revenue was considerably lower than originally anticipated.

Goldman Sachs also has suffered reverses in Russia. In early 1992, the Russian government appointed Goldman Sachs as advisor to the government on foreign investment. After internal bureaucratic conflict with respect to Goldman's role, the firm lost its support. The government's official position shifted to disapproval of Goldman for receiving fees from foreign companies and also acting as advisor to the Russian government on foreign investment. Goldman retrenched from Russia and is now conducting its Russian business from its Frankfurt office.

As a result of these expansionary moves, the staffing level at Goldman Sachs increased from 3,500 in the early 1980s to nearly 10,000 in the 1990s. Such rapid growth would have been impossible for any firm to manage. For Goldman Sachs, the difficulty was compounded by upheaval in the top ranks of management. In 1992, Robert Rubin left to become

economic advisor to the Clinton administration. On his departure, Stephen Friedman (the remaining cochairman) delayed
his retirement which had previously been planned for mid-
1993. Meanwhile, there had been little planning for his successor. Also troubling was the discovery by new partners that
the capital of the firm was eroding and that the leverage (debt
financing) was higher than the new partners previously had
anticipated. Suddenly, Friedman announced his retirement in
September 1994. With these developments, 35 general partners resigned and assumed limited partnerships.

These resignations and the eroding capital base as a
result of skyrocketing expenses led to a massive reconsider-
ation of Goldman Sachs' market positioning and management. Under the leadership of Jon Corzine, the new
chairman of Goldman Sachs, the firm is correcting many of
its past errors.

- Lax management is being replaced by better mechanisms for management succession, financial budget-
  ing, strategic planning, and risk control.
- The erosion of the collegial culture and resulting low
  morale are being addressed by (1) amendment of the
  compensation plan and (2) a focus on returning to
  traditional levels of profitability.
- Weak earnings and uncertainties with respect to the
  capital of the firm are being corrected by (1) removing excessive concentrations of risk, (2) diversifying
  and expanding in areas such as asset management
  and loan syndication, and (3) considering conversion
  to public ownership.
- Excessive costs are being contained by downsizing
  U.S. staff and reducing other expenses.
- Overemphasis on proprietary trading and investments is being replaced by a more traditional client
  orientation.
- The early retirements of vital partners is being
  addressed by attempts to persuade them to stay
  with the firm and expanding the size of the partnership.

The experience of Goldman Sachs is instructive for commercial banks for several reasons. Commercial banks have already embarked on major cost containment campaigns and, thus, generally have the management infrastructure for adequate corporate control. Commercial banks also have established good client relationships that will be key in the development of investment banking ties. Profitability in the banking industry is strong for the most part because of cost containment and product diversification. All of these factors suggest that commercial bank management is prepared to avoid many of the missteps of Goldman Sachs during the early 1990s.

At the same time, one element of investment banking may be more problematic for commercial-bankers-turned-investment-bankers. This issue is the inherently different corporate culture of a commercial bank versus an investment bank.

INVESTMENT BANKING CORPORATE CULTURE

Having been regulated in virtually every area of business, commercial bankers have established a hierarchy of command. In this sense, commercial banks in the United States and abroad tend to have bureaucratic forms of organization. On the other hand, investment banks are less bureaucratic and often more flexible.

Citicorp

In some cases, these cultural differences can prove difficult to overcome. At Citicorp, the commercial banking culture was characterized by three distinct groups—the consumer banking group, the corporate banking group, and the investment banking group. The consumer bank was extremely bureaucratic, characterized by long range, carefully crafted, predictable, and stable methods of operation. In this area, mass marketing, controlling costs, and standardized products were typical. The idea is that the successful consumer bank is subject to routine procedures that make it possible for managers at the top of the organization to determine the strategy, develop the creative work, and promote new products. Execution of these strategies is then hoped to be fairly effortless as it is only necessary to implement what has been created. Clearly, this is a top-down approach to banking.

In the corporate sector, Citibank's culture is geared toward long-term relationships with clients, fairly standardized products, and a structured approach to implementation. While less routine than consumer banking, the corporate banking sector of Citicorp was also fairly bureaucratic in nature.

On the other hand, the investment banking culture in Citicorp is much more short term and ad hoc in nature. Here, it is important to maintain a flexible organization that emphasizes deals rather than relationships. Some products themselves are designed especially for a specific transaction. Circumstances change very quickly and staff and resources must be able to do the same. Citicorp sometimes found that this quick-response capability created problems. There appeared to be a lack of a sense of loyalty and, often, a lack of banking and management skills.

Citicorp has managed to bridge the gap between these cultures by an overriding corporate culture. In general, Citicorp has always been an antiestablishment bank. It was founded in 1812 by New York businessmen dissatisfied with the service they received from the First Bank of the United States (founded by Alexander Hamilton). As an institution, Citicorp has consistently expanded with certain basic premises:

- A sense of entrepreneurship.
- A high tolerance for mistakes.
- An aversion for bureaucracy and centralization, historically encouraging managers to take initiatives on their own.
- A high degree of internal competition among individual managers who were encouraged to compete in the creation of new business.

- A meritocracy that valued talent and individual achievement.
- An activist and confrontational form of problem solving.
- Flexibility and institutional impatience, resulting in constant reorganization and personnel reassignment.

New management recruits to Citicorp learn early on that they are expected to take risks. In fact, they are informed that they will be penalized more severely for errors of omission than for errors of commission. John Reed, the bank's current chair, made mistakes in the consumer banking areas that cost the institution hundreds of millions of dollars. Walter Wriston, former chairman of Citicorp, tolerated these mistakes by Reed, continued to support him strongly, and never interrupted Reed's progression in the bank's management ranks.[3] In terms of permitting managers to support their own ideas, Citicorp has made it possible for new ideas to be supported by as much as $1 million on a completely experimental basis.

At the same time, Citicorp has encouraged its managers to compete with each other. One example is setting up very similar operations under three different managers and deciding, after 18 to 24 months, which manager was best suited to run the operation. A flexible, impatient management style results in the creation of multiple profit centers that can be likened to a perpetual hothouse of research and development. While Citicorp has faced a number of significant challenges, the institution has been able to blend the cultures of commercial and investment banking by encouraging the exploration of new approaches and ideas. Although every institution does not have the capital base or management depth of Citicorp, an openness for dialogue and consideration of all issues can be adopted by any institution.

J. P. Morgan

Perhaps at the other end of the spectrum is J. P. Morgan. After passage of Glass-Steagall in 1933, J. P. Morgan & Company divested itself of investment banking activities.

Over time, the bank maintained its elite clientele and strong reputation. The environment at J. P. Morgan was, and continues to be, much more stable than that of Citicorp. In fact, open debate is essentially discouraged. There is much more an aura of consensus building. Some of the management principles on which J. P. Morgan is built are

- Relationship banking and service to clients.
- High standards of professionalism and integrity.
- Strong emphasis on teamwork and collegiality (as opposed to individual star performers).
- Nonconfrontation and civility in internal relationships.
- Consensus decision making.
- Close relationship between the bank and its employees, evidenced by extensive services and perks, unparalleled management training, job rotation, and a long process of socializing employees to the "Morgan way of doing things."
- Close attention to detail in both strategic and day-to-day administrative matters.

J. P. Morgan made the transition to merchant and investment banking beginning in 1980. At that time, fee income was a low 12 to 15 percent of gross revenue. Eight years later, this percentage was up to 47 percent; by 1990 it was more than 60 percent. J. P. Morgan managed this transition by becoming a simpler, more informal organization as compared to previous years. Morgan's new functional structure is similar to product divisions of non- financial firms. In preparation for the repeal of Glass-Steagall, Morgan has also set up a number of subsidiaries (some still only shell organizations), initiated capital markets training, and conducted global markets seminars. Former geographic area managers have been eliminated. Specialists in product lines report to functional divisional heads instead of the former geographic region managers. Specifically, there are seven business groups and nine support groups. The business groups are

1. Securities sales and trading.
2. Corporate finance and mergers and acquisitions.
3. Operations services.
4. Euroclear (clearing of European securities transactions).
5. Private banking.
6. Investment management.
7. Equity investment.

The support groups are

1. Human resources.
2. Auditing.
3. Financial services.
4. Credit policy.
5. Global support systems.
6. Nonbank subsidiaries.
7. Research.
8. Legal and corporate staff.
9. Other branch and subsidiary staff.

Certain changes have been necessary within Morgan to effect these changes and to progress in the transition. Specifically, each division is now more profit centered. Morgan now has a more aggressive and competitive posture in the financial marketplace. There is more emphasis on pay for performance. Faster decision making is now being emphasized. Lastly, some of the conservatism with respect to cost control has been relaxed, enabling managers to invest in the necessary infrastructure of new buildings, technology, and staff that are required to become an aggressive global competitor.

Success in combining the cultures of commercial and investment banking appears to be linked to the willingness to change. Recognizing that there are differences in culture is the first step. Then, developing a common set of goals and objectives follows. Lastly, doing those things necessary to effect these goals and objectives is critical.

THE MOVEMENT TOWARD
FUND MANAGEMENT

In the future, commercial banks will increasingly move into the area of fund management. This is a continuing process that began primarily with (1) third-party funds being offered to bank customers or (2) the conversion of some trust department assets into publicly available funds.

PNC Mutual Funds

PNC Bank Corporation and its affiliates constitute one of the country's largest bank managers of mutual funds. PNC Institutional Management Corporation (PIMC), a subsidiary of PNC Bank, is the investment advisor to the PNC family of funds. These funds are available at PNC Bank locations through PNC Brokerage Corporation, PNC Securities Corporation, and PNC investment management and trust.[4]

One of the newer funds offered by PNC is the International Emerging Markets Fund. This fund focuses on companies in various geographic regions throughout the world and selects those that appear to be undervalued. The selection process is geared toward stocks with a relatively low price-to-earnings ratio and price-to-cash-flow ratio. The selection of these stocks is not based on any regional considerations. Instead, the investment advisor for the fund, PIMC, looks to specific companies in new and expanding markets. The objective is long-term capital appreciation and portfolio diversification.

Another recent addition to the PNC Family of Funds is the International Dollar Reserve Fund I (IDR). The international nature of the IDR is distinguished from that of the International Emerging Markets Fund. IDR is a dollar-denominated money market fund for non-U.S. citizens and for institutions acting on behalf of clients who are not U.S. persons (as defined by the Internal Revenue Code). IDR is a purely offshore investment vehicle. Its income is not subject to U.S. income taxes; it provides monthly income and cash flow to shareholders; it provides portfolio diversification; and it has the advantage of same-day settlement. Essentially, IDR is a money-market mutual fund in these non-U.S. instruments:

- Certificates of deposit.
- Bankers' acceptances, time deposits issued or supported by credit of non-U.S. banks, some non-U.S. branches of non-U.S. banks, and some non-U.S. branches of U.S. banks.
- Commercial paper, loan participation interest, notes, bonds, and other instruments issued or guaranteed by non-U.S. corporations or other non-U.S. entities.
- Obligations of supranational entities including world institutions and organizations.
- Obligations issued or guaranteed by governments and governmental subdivisions, excluding the United States.
- Variable- or floating-rate notes of non-U.S. issuers.
- Repurchase agreements from non-U.S. institutions.

These fund offerings by PNC illustrate the extent to which regional U.S. banks are becoming involved in securities transactions and the extent to which these transactions are international in scope. This trend also will increase in the future. The search for diversification and for yield will cause commercial banks investment banking activities to become more integrated into the international financial system. The family of funds offered by PNC also illustrates the increasing variety of securities activities in which commercial banks will be involved. The PNC family of funds includes:

- PNC Balanced Portfolio.
- PNC Index Equity Portfolio.
- PNC Value Equity Portfolio.
- PNC SmallCap Growth Equity Portfolio.
- PNC Growth Equity Portfolio.

- PNC International Equity Portfolio.
- PNC Money-Market Portfolio.
- PNC Government Money-Market Portfolio.
- PNC Ohio Municipal Market Funds.
- PNC Tax-Free Money-Market Portfolio.
- PNC Intermediate Government Portfolio.
- PNC Managed Income Portfolio.
- PNC Tax-Free Income Portfolio.
- PNC Ohio Tax-Free Income Portfolio.
- PNC Core Equity Portfolio.
- PNC Pennsylvania Tax-Free Income Portfolio.
- PNC Short-Term Bond Portfolio.
- PNC Intermediate-Term Bond Portfolio.
- PNC Municipal Money-Market Portfolio.
- PNC Pennsylvania Municipal Money-Market Port-folio.
- PNC Virginia Municipal Money-Market Portfolio.
- PNC Government Income Portfolio.

Mellon Bank, the Boston Co., and Dreyfus Corporation

Instead of initiating and growing mutual funds *de novo*, it is possible for a bank to purchase an existing family of funds. Mellon Bank has taken this approach in the 1993 purchase of the Boston Co. and the 1994 acquisition of Dreyfus.

Immediately before the acquisition of Boston Co., the firm managed mutual funds in the amount of $50 billion for Shearson, a division of American Express. This activity alone generated $100 million per year in revenues. The fees were generally higher than the going market rate. However, because American Express also owned Boston Co., the high fees were not an issue. Then American Express sold Boston Co. to Mellon Bank and Shearson to Primerica, now known as the Travelers. Shortly after both sales were consummated, Primerica balked at the high fees charged by

Boston Co., but no agreement was reached by Boston Co. and Primerica to lower them. In retaliation, Primerica set up clones of the Shearson funds and attempted to persuade investors to switch. Mellon Bank sued Primerica; this suit was settled in January 1994. However, Mellon was forced to accept lower fees for managing the funds and the market reacted negatively to the controversy fearing that assets under management would be severely depleted. As a result, the value of Mellon stock fell.

When interest rates began to rise in February 1994, senior management at Mellon Bank became concerned that losses would be incurred at the Boston Co. Frank Cahoet, CEO of Mellon, pressured Desmond Heathwood, chairman of Boston Co. Asset Management (BCAM), into restructuring a portfolio that was heavily laden with derivatives. As a result of the restructuring, a $130 million charge was incurred in the fourth quarter of 1994. Heathwood vehemently felt that the restructuring was unnecessary and ill-advised. Apparently, Heathwood also was displeased with certain aspects of Mellon Bank's management of the securities affiliate. Examples that highlight the frugal nature of Mellon's rules include an allocation of only $5 per employee for BCAM's Christmas party, removing parking privileges (as is the case throughout Mellon Bank), and the personal review by the Mellon Bank CEO of all employee salary increases for staff earning in excess of $40,000.

Heathwood was so displeased by these developments that he left Boston Co. and started a rival firm, Boston Partners Asset Management LP. Within three months of his departure, 30 former Boston Co. co-workers had joined the new firm and $3.5 billion of the $26 billion of BCAM assets had been transferred to Boston Partners Asset Management.

The Dreyfus acquisition has not fared much better in the early years. For its part, Dreyfus Corporation (based in New York) had $80 billion of assets under management (prior to the acquisition). The December 1993 announcement of the acquisition promised to increase fees for the consolidated Mellon Bank considerably. In fact, Mellon would become the largest bank manager of mutual funds by a wide margin. The new division of the combined company would serve as a financial-services powerhouse for the broad investing public.

Then interest rates began to rise in February 1994. Dreyfus was caught by the same downdraft that affected the entire mutual fund industry. In addition, the more lax management style at Dreyfus has clashed with the more bureaucratic management style of Mellon Bank. Mellon has sharply curtailed compensation, expenditures for new initiatives, and other costs. The combination of these factors appears to be taking its toll. Jay DeMartine, the former head of Dreyfus Marketing, resigned his position in December 1994, only nine months after assuming the new post. In addition, scores of analysts and back-room personnel have left the firm. Most notably, Dreyfus has lost $10 billion, or 12.5 percent, of assets under management. Its market share declined from 3.7 percent in December 1993 to 3.1 percent by October 1994. Morale within the organization is reportedly low.

Mellon Bank has had unfortunate experiences in its acquisitions to increase its presence in the fund management field. Nevertheless, such acquisitions will be a strong trend of the future. The challenge for commercial banks will be to manage the process without disrupting the functioning of the acquired subsidiary and create circumstances that reduce the market value of the bank's own stock. This can be achieved only by an open and frank assessment of the challenges to integrating the two cultures of a commercial bank and a securities operation. Then, reasonable, negotiated policy decisions can be made to maximize the vast potential for increased fee income and shareholder value.

PRIVATE EQUITY ISSUES

Another increasing trend is the issuance of private equity. In a private equity issue, individual investors and financiers are willing to commit significant minority equity capital to well-managed firms that have attractive long-term prospects. Warren Buffett, chairman of Berkshire Hathaway, is perhaps the best example of such an investor. During the late 1980s, several firms began to create an institutional framework through which private equity issues could be launched. This framework involved special-purpose limited partnerships that provided equity capital to medium-size companies on a noncontrolling basis.

The development of private equity issues is, in a sense, an adaptation of large financial institutions outside the United States that had been primary sources of private equity investment into fast growing companies. Japan and Germany are good examples. In both countries, financial institutions hold equity stakes in companies. In Japan, equity stakes often are held in *keiretsu* members. These affiliated companies have strategic and financial ties. In Germany, the *hausbank* is the bank primarily responsible for financing for a given firm; it provides advisory services, as well as long-term debt and equity financial support.

The development of a limited-purpose investment company, however, is an innovation of the United States. Private equity issuances in the United States raised $12 billion in 1994 as compared to $36 billion in the initial public offering (IPO) market during the same year. Furthermore, the 1994 volume in the IPO market was 37 percent less than the 1993 total of IPSs. Nevertheless, certain advantages are associated with a private equity issue:

- The *confidentiality* of the arrangement is useful if the funds are being raised for an acquisition.
- The *speed* of a response means that private investors may be tapped quickly as compared to the registration process associated with an IPO.
- Issuers know with *certainty* the price and volume of the issue.
- Even though private equity issues tend to be more expensive, *pricing* can be relatively attractive if there is sufficient investor interest.
- Issuers associate a certain *prestige* with the confidence implied by a direct private equity investment.

For example, Columbia Hospital/HCA Healthcare Corporation (Columbia HCA) needed to raise $40 million in new equity. However, it was not completely confident that this equity could be raised in a public issue. Today, Columbia HCA is the largest operator of acute-care hospitals in the United States and has a market capitalization of more than $13 billion. At the time of its 1991 capital raising, five factors suggested the company would have difficulty in the public markets. First, Columbia HCA was not well known, even though it was a public company. It had gone public as a result of a reverse merger with Smith Laboratories. In its own right, Smith was not a well-known company. The reverse merger left Columbia HCA without the traditional roadshow to educate investors about a company that was essentially a cash-rich holding company. Second, the historical financial results of Columbia HCA were not comparable because of the reverse merger and its 1990 earnings per share were depressed because of accounting for shares issued to principal owners and operators. Third, Columbia HCA did not have a track record of operating acquired hospitals and the practice of physician ownership was still controversial. Fourth, Columbia HCA was on the verge of closing two important hospital acquisitions which it preferred not to disclose until the transactions were finalized. Lastly, the Gulf War in 1991 had depressed the activity of new stock issuances in general.

Thus, in March 1991 Columbia HCA issued a $40 million convertible security to the 1818 Funds and closed the acquisitions of the two Florida hospitals. Over the following six months, Columbia HCA completed public common and subordinated note issues.

The 1818 Fund is managed by Brown Brothers Harriman & Company. There are two versions of the enterprise—The 1818 Fund, LP and the 1818 Fund II, LP. Both funds were founded in 1989 and have raised $800 million in capital commitments to make negotiated investments in public and private companies. The equity needs typically range between $25 million and $75 million. These funds have invested in 12 public and private companies and have substantial resources still available for investment.

Other funds have been created for similar purposes. For example, J. P. Morgan & Company is a shareholder in Trident Corporation, a $663 million partnership that makes private investments in the insurance industry. A consortium that includes Morgan Stanley Capital Partners purchased Nokia Aluminum from the mobile telephone manufacturer of the same name in December 1994. Goldman Sachs, through GS Capital Partners, is one of the largest private equity investors for startup capital. Firms that have received capital from GS Capital Partners include Diamond Cable (a U.K. television company) and Polo Ralph Lauren.

In addition to these examples in the United States and the United Kingdom, private equity is being made available to firms throughout the developed and developing world. Examples include the Czech Republic, Russia, and Chile. Private equity issues offer another alternative to participating in investment banking activities and are an excellent way for medium-size firms to receive investment banking services—either distribution or investment—from medium-size institutions. The use of private equity will increase in the future.

INTERNATIONAL CONNECTIONS

The capital markets of the United States are an attractive incentive for foreign institutions to enter investment banking in the United States. In addition, U.S. institutions will look abroad increasingly to expand their investment banking activities as their clients become more involved in international trade and investment. In addition, outside the mature U.S. market, growth potential is strongest in some of the emerging economies.

Deutsche Bank

The U.S. affiliate of Germany's Deutsche Bank is implementing a strategy to become a major force in U.S. investment banking. Germany's largest bank has hired top-flight capital markets professionals from New York firms, offering generous compensation packages and guarantees. It appears that the bank is committed to do whatever is required to recruit the top talent in the city. Deutsche Bank hired the top manager of a capital markets group of Merrill Lynch and subsequently hired away the manager's successor at Merrill Lynch, raiding the firm twice in the same department. Citibank was hit by Deutsche Bank when it lured away its best group of foreign exchange specialists. These efforts have not been restricted to U.S. firms, however. S.G. Warburg lost its merger and acquisition staff to the bank.

Deutsche Bank also is buying entire divisions and setting up strategic alliances to strengthen its investment banking presence. Deutsche Bank recently purchased ITT's commercial finance unit for $868 million to become a major force in the asset-backed securities market. Also, the bank has a fee-sharing arrangement with Gretcher & Co., a merger and acquisition advisory firm. As soon as the Federal Reserve approves the transaction, Deutsche Bank will acquire a 25 percent stake in Gretcher. Deutsche Bank is clearly attempting to become the most powerful universal bank in the world.

These efforts follow what is certainly an embarrassing setback for the huge institution. The privatization of Bavaria's electric utility was awarded to Lehman Brothers instead of Deutsche Bank in 1994. While German banks still handle the majority of investment banking deals in Germany, U.S. firms are capturing respectable shares in the German market. The shift began in 1990 with German reunification. The need for financing was tremendous and U.S. investment banks helped fill the need. Since that time, a number of privatizations, mergers, and stock offerings have been won by U.S. firms. In the area of futures and options trading on the Frankfurt Stock Exchange, U.S. firms have a very strong presence.

J. P. Morgan is one of several U.S. banks that have been successful in German investment management, overseeing DM4.3 billion for German banks and corporations since establishing its presence in 1991. Goldman Sachs recently won the mandate for the largest privatization in

Germany, if not the world, for Deutsche Telekom AG. In addition to the mandate for Germany's largest telephone company, Goldman orchestrated Germany's first leveraged buyout—Tarkett International, a floor products company.

Under the circumstances, the aggressive reaction of Deutsche Bank is perhaps understandable. The objective is to become a truly global investment bank, understanding that such a definition cannot apply to an institution without a strong investment banking presence in the United States. The bank aspires to become one of the top global swap dealers and one of the three leading foreign exchange traders. Of course, there will be stiff competition from U.S. firms in New York. Also working to the disadvantage of Deutsche Bank is its relatively weak U.S. securities distribution capability. The bank has relatively few relationships with U.S.-domiciled companies. A major challenge for the bank also will be its historical aversion to risk and its extensive (some say cumbersome) control and audit procedures.

At the same time, Deutsche Bank has several advantages in its quest for investment banking greatness. The mark is strong and the dollar is weak, giving the bank a financial advantage. Deutsche Bank already has close ties with many European multinational corporations; this can be an advantage for the bank in its dealings with U.S. affiliates of the multinationals. Perhaps its greatest strength, however, is its top credit rating and its huge capital base, both of which will help Deutsche Bank to (1) receive top credit ratings for underwriting clients and (2) retain top talent and resources to give the best possible service.

NationsBank

NationsBank is an example of a U.S. bank that is expanding in investment banking activities and international enterprises at the same time. As the third largest institution in the United States, NationsBank has grown rapidly in less than a decade. With its Section 20 subsidiary, NationsBank is now underwriting $15 billion in corporate debt per year. With this type of activity, Nations-

Bank is becoming less of a super-regional and more of a money-center bank. Among some of the transactions that NationsBank has undertaken:

- Global arranger of a $20.6 billion revolving credit facility for General Motors Acceptance Corporation.
- Lead manager of a $1.5 billion revolving credit facility for Turner Broadcasting System.
- Sole provider of a $500 million interest rate swap and swaptions package for Time Warner.

Clearly continued growth will necessitate an expansion into international markets. The Southeast region, home territory for NationsBank (Charlotte, North Carolina), is considered the most important regional recipient of foreign direct investment in the United States. This is primarily attributable to the relatively low cost of doing business and a solid infrastructure. An estimated 2,000 foreign companies are now invested in the Southeast region, representing $32 billion in invested capital and 356,000 employees. Thus, NationsBank has an appreciation for the impact of foreign trade and investment.

The Chicago Research and Trading Group (CRT), NationsBank's derivatives market-making and trading firm, already operates in London. In 1995, CRT set up a branch in Hong Kong, followed in short order by a Nations-Bank office. The Hong Kong operations will help provide project finance in power generation, transportation, and telecommunications for U.S. clients in Asia.

As the mutual fund asset management arm of Nations-Bank, NationsFund is second only to Mellon Bank (with its Dreyfus affiliation) with $16 billion under management. In addition, the bank manages $56 billion in trust assets. Recognizing that proper diversification required international investment of some of these funds, the bank elected to buy instead of build expertise in international investment. In November 1994, NationsBank entered a 50/50 joint venture with Gartmore Capital Management, a $32 billion London-based international investment house owned by Banque Indosuez. The joint venture, Nations Gartmore Investment

Management, operates out of London with an initial capital base of approximately $1 billion. The current objective is to become actively invested in the Pacific Rim's emerging markets and the global market for fixed-income securities. By the turn of the century, the objective is to have $5 billion under international management.

NationsBank symbolizes the kind of growth opportunities realized by U.S. banks that enter the securities field. This will be a trend of the future, particularly U.S. banks forming strategic alliances with overseas firms of comparable size and/or compatible characteristics.

THE TRANSFORMATION

The U.S. commercial banking industry will be transformed by some factors outside its control and by other factors it will orchestrate. Outside the control of the industry are the competitive forces it has faced for many years. Also outside the industry's control is the volatility of interest rates and economic conditions.

Those factors falling within the control of the industry include product mix and targeted customers. There appears to be little doubt that the future product mix of commercial banks must include securities-related services. Without this feature, commercial banks will find themselves increasingly on the sidelines in the financial services arena. Indeed, a basic product of commercial banks—the loan—is becoming raw material for the production of new, securitized assets. With the reduction (and eventual elimination) of Glass-Steagall restrictions of commercial banks in the securities industry, the choice is varied—underwriting bonds (Treasury, municipal, or corporate), underwriting stock (public or private), or offering proprietary mutual funds. In any event, the commercial bank looking for growth markets will select at least one of these areas in which to expand. As U.S. markets continue to mature, a number of institutions will look for growth overseas. Whether the international connection is an acquisition or a strategic alliance, this trend will be a natural outgrowth.

The involvement of commercial banks in investment banking is, itself, a natural outgrowth. Banks have a competitive advantage in the area of credit analysis, large capital bases, and significant placing power in the form of existing clients (if developed). When the two industries are once again allowed to develop in an unencumbered, pre-Glass-Steagall sense, both industries will thrive and improved financing alternatives will facilitate continued economic growth for the United States.

SELECTED REFERENCES

Ball, Matthew. "Attracting the Private Buyer to Your Equity." *Corporate Finance*, February 1995, pp. 40–44.

Lee, Peter. "All Change (Securities Markets)." *Euromoney*, June 1994, pp. 89–101.

Lee, Peter. "Which Is the Real Goldman Sachs?" *Euromoney*, October 1993, pp. 50–57.

Paré, Terence P. "A Bitter Lesson for Banks (Mellon Bank)." *Fortune*, August 21, 1995, pp. 54–55.

Raghavan, Anita. "Merchant Banks Become Profit Centers." *The Wall Street Journal*, February 23, 1995, pp. C1 and C11.

Rogers, David. *The Future of American Banking.* New York: McGraw-Hill, 1993.

Sprio, Leah Nathans. "A Brutal Morning After: How Bad Is Wall Street's Headache?" *Business Week*, October 31, 1994, pp. 40–43.

Stewart, Jules. "Not a Lender But a Borrower Be." *Euromoney*, September 1995, pp. 269–70.

Tucker, Lawrence, and Michael Long. "Why a Private Offering Pays." *Corporate Finance*, October 1994, pp. 32–35.

"When the Tough Get Going (America's Investment Banks)." *The Economist*, October 22, 1994, pp. 89–90.

Wright, Rob. "Grow or Go (NationsBank)." *The Banker*, February 1995, pp. 20–21.

Zweig, Phillip L. "Deutsche Bank Goes on the Attack." *Business Week*, July 17, 1995, pp. 83–84.

Zweig, Phillip L.; Rose Brady; David Lindorff; and Paula Dwyer. "Where Does Goldman Sachs Go From Here?" *Business Week*, March 20, 1995, pp. 104–10.

Zweig, Phillip L.; Kelley Holland; and Keith Alexander. "Tense Scenes from a Marriage (Mellon-Dreyfus)." *Business Week*, January 16, 1995, pp. 66–67.

ENDNOTES

1. See Chapter 2 for a discussion of bulge bracket firms and the underwriting syndicate.

2. Merchant banking involves a bank that arranges credit financing but does not hold loans to maturity. Typically, a merchant bank invests in leveraged buyouts, corporate acquisitions, and other structured finance transactions.

3. The mistakes of John Reed included indiscriminate mailing of credit cards to uncreditworthy individuals, a large position

in fixed-rate mortgages just before interest rates increased significantly, and installation of an expensive computer system that did not function well and was abandoned after two years.

4. Recall that PNC Securities Corporation is a Section 20 subsidiary (see Chapter 4).

Present and Future Value Tables

T A B L E   A-1

Future Value of $1
$FVIF = (1 + k)^n$

PERIODS	1%	2%	3%	4%	5%	6%
1	1.0100	1.0200	1.0300	1.0400	1.0500	1.0600
2	1.0201	1.0404	1.0609	1.0816	1.1025	1.1236
3	1.0303	1.0612	1.0927	1.1249	1.1576	1.1910
4	1.0406	1.0824	1.1255	1.1699	1.2155	1.2625
5	1.0510	1.1041	1.1593	1.2167	1.2763	1.3382
6	1.0615	1.1262	1.1941	1.2653	1.3401	1.4185
7	1.0721	1.1487	1.2299	1.3159	1.4071	1.5036
8	1.0829	1.1717	1.2668	1.3686	1.4775	1.5938
9	1.0937	1.1951	1.3048	1.4233	1.5513	1.6895
10	1.1046	1.2190	1.3439	1.4802	1.6289	1.7908
11	1.1157	1.2434	1.3842	1.5395	1.7103	1.8983
12	1.1268	1.2682	1.4258	1.6010	1.7959	2.0122
13	1.1381	1.2936	1.4685	1.6651	1.8856	2.1329
14	1.1495	1.3195	1.5126	1.7317	1.9799	2.2609
15	1.1610	1.3459	1.5580	1.8009	2.0789	2.3966
16	1.1726	1.3728	1.6047	1.8730	2.1829	2.5404
17	1.1843	1.4002	1.6528	1.9479	2.2920	2.6928
18	1.1961	1.4282	1.7024	2.0258	2.4066	2.8543
19	1.2081	1.4568	1.7535	2.1068	2.5270	3.0256
20	1.2202	1.4859	1.8061	2.1911	2.6533	3.2071
25	1.2824	1.6406	2.0938	2.6658	3.3864	4.2919
30	1.3478	1.8114	2.4273	3.2434	4.3219	5.7435
35	1.4166	1.9999	2.8139	3.9461	5.5160	7.6861
40	1.4889	2.2080	3.2620	4.8010	7.0400	10.2857
45	1.5648	2.4379	3.7816	5.8412	8.9850	13.7646
50	1.6446	2.6916	4.3839	7.1067	11.4674	18.4202

T A B L E A–1 *Continued*

PERIODS	7%	8%	9%	10%	11%	12%	13%
1	1.0700	1.0800	1.0900	1.1000	1.1100	1.1200	1.1300
2	1.1449	1.1664	1.1881	1.2100	1.2321	1.2544	1.2769
3	1.2250	1.2597	1.2950	1.3310	1.3676	1.4049	1.4429
4	1.3108	1.3605	1.4116	1.4641	1.5181	1.5735	1.6305
5	1.4026	1.4693	1.5386	1.6105	1.6851	1.7623	1.8424
6	1.5007	1.5869	1.6771	1.7716	1.8704	1.9738	2.0820
7	1.6058	1.7138	1.8280	1.9487	2.0762	2.2107	2.3526
8	1.7182	1.8509	1.9926	2.1436	2.3045	2.4760	2.6584
9	1.8385	1.9990	2.1719	2.3579	2.5580	2.7731	3.0040
10	1.9672	2.1589	2.3674	2.5937	2.8394	3.1058	3.3946
11	2.1049	2.3316	2.5804	2.8531	3.1518	3.4785	3.8359
12	2.2522	2.5182	2.8127	3.1384	3.4985	3.8960	4.3345
13	2.4098	2.7196	3.0658	3.4523	3.8833	4.3635	4.8980
14	2.5785	2.9372	3.3417	3.7975	4.3104	4.8871	5.5348
15	2.7590	3.1722	3.6425	4.1772	4.7846	5.4736	6.2543
16	2.9522	3.4259	3.9703	4.5950	5.3109	6.1304	7.0673
17	3.1588	3.7000	4.3276	5.0545	5.8951	6.8660	7.9861
18	3.3799	3.9960	4.7171	5.5599	6.5436	7.6900	9.0243
19	3.6165	4.3157	5.1417	6.1159	7.2633	8.6128	10.1974
20	3.8697	4.6610	5.6044	6.7275	8.0623	9.6463	11.5231
25	5.4274	6.8485	8.6231	10.8347	13.5855	17.0001	21.2305
30	7.6123	10.0627	13.2677	17.4494	22.8923	29.9599	39.1159
35	10.6766	14.7853	20.4140	28.1024	38.5749	52.7996	72.0685
40	14.9745	21.7245	31.4094	45.2593	65.0009	93.0510	132.7816
45	21.0025	31.9204	48.3273	72.8905	109.5302	163.9876	244.6414
50	29.4570	46.9016	74.3575	117.3909	184.5648	289.0022	450.7359

T A B L E A–1 *Concluded*

PERIODS	14%	15%	16%	17%	18%	19%	20%
1	1.1400	1.1500	1.1600	1.1700	1.1800	1.1900	1.2000
2	1.2996	1.3225	1.3456	1.3689	1.3924	1.4161	1.4400
3	1.4815	1.5209	1.5609	1.6016	1.6430	1.6852	1.7280
4	1.6890	1.7490	1.8106	1.8739	1.9388	2.0053	2.0736
5	1.9254	2.0114	2.1003	2.1924	2.2878	2.3864	2.4883
6	2.1950	2.3131	2.4364	2.5652	2.6996	2.8398	2.9860
7	2.5023	2.6600	2.8262	3.0012	3.1855	3.3793	3.5832
8	2.8526	3.0590	3.2784	3.5115	3.7589	4.0214	4.2998
9	3.2519	3.5179	3.8030	4.1084	4.4355	4.7854	5.1598
10	3.7072	4.0456	4.4114	4.8068	5.2338	5.6947	6.1917
11	4.2262	4.6524	5.1173	5.6240	6.1759	6.7767	7.4301
12	4.8179	5.3503	5.9360	6.5801	7.2876	8.0642	8.9161
13	5.4924	6.1528	6.8858	7.6987	8.5994	9.5964	10.6993
14	6.2613	7.0757	7.9875	9.0075	10.1472	11.4198	12.8392
15	7.1379	8.1371	9.2655	10.5387	11.9737	13.5895	15.4070
16	8.1372	9.3576	10.7480	12.3303	14.1290	16.1715	18.4884
17	9.2765	10.7613	12.4677	14.4265	16.6722	19.2441	22.1861
18	10.5752	12.3755	14.4625	16.8790	19.6733	22.9005	26.6233
19	12.0557	14.2318	16.7765	19.7484	23.2144	27.2516	31.9480
20	13.7435	16.3665	19.4608	23.1056	27.3930	32.4294	38.3376
25	26.4619	32.9190	40.8742	50.6578	62.6686	77.3881	95.3962
30	50.9502	66.2118	85.8499	111.0647	143.3706	184.6753	237.3763
35	98.1002	133.1755	180.3141	243.5035	327.9973	440.7006	590.6682
40	188.8835	267.8635	378.7212	533.8687	750.3783	1.05e+03	1.47e+03
45	363.6791	538.7693	795.4438	1.17e+03	1.72e+03	2.51e+03	3.66e+03
50	700.2330	1.08e+03	1.67e+03	2.57e+03	3.93e+03	5.99e+03	9.10e+03

T A B L E A-2

Future Value of an Annuity of $1
$FVIFA = ((1 + k)^n - 1)/k$

PERIODS	1%	2%	3%	4%	5%	6%
1	1.0000	1.0000	1.0000	1.0000	1.0000	1.0000
2	2.0100	2.0200	2.0300	2.0400	2.0500	2.0600
3	3.0301	3.0604	3.0909	3.1216	3.1525	3.1836
4	4.0604	4.1216	4.1836	4.2465	4.3101	4.3746
5	5.1010	5.2040	5.3091	5.4163	5.5256	5.6371
6	6.1520	6.3081	6.4684	6.6330	6.8019	6.9753
7	7.2135	7.4343	7.6625	7.8983	8.1420	8.3938
8	8.2857	8.5830	8.8923	9.2142	9.5491	9.8975
9	9.3685	9.7546	10.1591	10.5828	11.0266	11.4913
10	10.4622	10.9497	11.4639	12.0061	12.5779	13.1808
11	11.5668	12.1687	12.8078	13.4864	14.2068	14.9716
12	12.6825	13.4121	14.1920	15.0258	15.9171	16.8699
13	13.8093	14.6803	15.6178	16.6268	17.7130	18.8821
14	14.9474	15.9739	17.0863	18.2919	19.5986	21.0151
15	16.0969	17.2934	18.5989	20.0236	21.5786	23.2760
16	17.2579	18.6393	20.1569	21.8245	23.6575	25.6725
17	18.4304	20.0121	21.7616	23.6975	25.8404	28.2129
18	19.6147	21.4123	23.4144	25.6454	28.1324	30.9057
19	20.8109	22.8406	25.1169	27.6712	30.5390	33.7600
20	22.0190	24.2974	26.8704	29.7781	33.0660	36.7856
25	28.2432	32.0303	36.4593	41.6459	47.7271	54.8645
30	34.7849	40.5681	47.5754	56.0849	66.4388	79.0582
35	41.6603	49.9945	60.4621	73.6522	90.3203	111.4348
40	48.8864	60.4020	75.4013	95.0255	120.7998	154.7620
45	56.4811	71.8927	92.7199	121.0294	159.7002	212.7435
50	64.4632	84.5794	112.7969	152.6671	209.3480	290.3359

T A B L E   A–2 *Continued*

PERIODS	7%	8%	9%	10%	11%	12%	13%
1	1.0000	1.0000	1.0000	1.0000	1.0000	1.0000	1.0000
2	2.0700	2.0800	2.0900	2.1000	2.1100	2.1200	2.1300
3	3.2149	3.2464	3.2781	3.3100	3.3421	3.3744	3.4069
4	4.4399	4.5061	4.5731	4.6410	4.7097	4.7793	4.8498
5	5.7507	5.8666	5.9847	6.1051	6.2278	6.3528	6.4803
6	7.1533	7.3359	7.5233	7.7156	7.9129	8.1152	8.3227
7	8.6540	8.9228	9.2004	9.4872	9.7833	10.0890	10.4047
8	10.2598	10.6366	11.0285	11.4359	11.8594	12.2997	12.7573
9	11.9780	12.4876	13.0210	13.5795	14.1640	14.7757	15.4157
10	13.8164	14.4866	15.1929	15.9374	16.7220	17.5487	18.4197
11	15.7836	16.6455	17.5603	18.5312	19.5614	20.6546	21.8143
12	17.8885	18.9771	20.1407	21.3843	22.7132	24.1331	25.6502
13	20.1406	21.4953	22.9534	24.5227	26.2116	28.0291	29.9847
14	22.5505	24.2149	26.0192	27.9750	30.0949	32.3926	34.8827
15	25.1290	27.1521	29.3609	31.7725	34.4054	37.2797	40.4175
16	27.8881	30.3243	33.0034	35.9497	39.1899	42.7533	46.6717
17	30.8402	33.7502	36.9737	40.5447	44.5008	48.8837	53.7391
18	33.9990	37.4502	41.3013	45.5992	50.3959	55.7497	61.7251
19	37.3790	41.4463	46.0185	51.1591	56.9395	63.4397	70.7494
20	40.9955	45.7620	51.1601	57.2750	64.2028	72.0524	80.9468
25	63.2490	73.1059	84.7009	98.3471	114.4133	133.3339	155.6196
30	94.4608	113.2832	136.3075	164.4940	199.0209	241.3327	293.1992
35	138.2369	172.3168	215.7108	271.0244	341.5896	431.6635	546.6808
40	199.6351	259.0565	337.8824	442.5926	581.8261	767.0914	1.01e+03
45	285.7493	386.5056	525.8587	718.9048	986.6386	1.36e+03	1.87e+03
50	406.5289	573.7702	815.0836	1.16e+03	1.67e+03	2.40e+03	3.46e+03

T A B L E A-2 *Concluded*

PERIODS	14%	15%	16%	17%	18%	19%	20%
1	1.0000	1.0000	1.0000	1.0000	1.0000	1.0000	1.0000
2	2.1400	2.1500	2.1600	2.1700	2.1800	2.1900	2.2000
3	3.4396	3.4725	3.5056	3.5389	3.5724	3.6061	3.6400
4	4.9211	4.9934	5.0665	5.1405	5.2154	5.2913	5.3680
5	6.6101	6.7424	6.8771	7.0144	7.1542	7.2966	7.4416
6	8.5355	8.7537	8.9775	9.2068	9.4420	9.6830	9.9299
7	10.7305	11.0668	11.4139	11.7720	12.1415	12.5227	12.9159
8	13.2328	13.7268	14.2401	14.7733	15.3270	15.9020	16.4991
9	16.0853	16.7858	17.5185	18.2847	19.0859	19.9234	20.7989
10	19.3373	20.3037	21.3215	22.3931	23.5213	24.7089	25.9587
11	23.0445	24.3493	25.7329	27.1999	28.7551	30.4035	32.1504
12	27.2707	29.0017	30.8502	32.8239	34.9311	37.1802	39.5805
13	32.0887	34.3519	36.7862	39.4040	42.2187	45.2445	48.4966
14	37.5811	40.5047	43.6720	47.1027	50.8180	54.8409	59.1959
15	43.8424	47.5804	51.6595	56.1101	60.9653	66.2607	72.0351
16	50.9804	55.7175	60.9250	66.6488	72.9390	79.8502	87.4421
17	59.1176	65.0751	71.6730	78.9792	87.0680	96.0218	105.9306
18	68.3941	75.8364	84.1407	93.4056	103.7403	115.2659	128.1167
19	78.9692	88.2118	98.6032	110.2846	123.4135	138.1664	154.7400
20	91.0249	102.4436	115.3797	130.0329	146.6280	165.4180	186.6880
25	181.8708	212.7930	249.2140	292.1049	342.6035	402.0425	471.9811
30	356.7868	434.7451	530.3117	647.4391	790.9480	966.7122	1.18e+03
35	693.5727	881.1702	1.12e+03	1.43e+03	1.82e+03	2.31e+03	2.95e+03
40	1.34e+03	1.78e+03	2.36e+03	3.13e+03	4.16e+03	5.53e+03	7.34e+03
45	2.59e+03	3.59e+03	4.97e+03	6.88e+03	9.53e+03	1.32e+04	1.83e+04
50	4.99e+03	7.22e+03	1.04e+04	1.51e+04	2.18e+04	3.15e+04	4.55e+04

T A B L E A–3

Present Value of $1
$PVIF = (1/ (1 + k)^n)$

PERIODS	1%	2%	3%	4%	5%	6%
1	0.9901	0.9804	0.9709	0.9615	0.9524	0.9434
2	0.9803	0.9612	0.9426	0.9246	0.9070	0.8900
3	0.9706	0.9423	0.9151	0.8890	0.8638	0.8396
4	0.9610	0.9238	0.8885	0.8548	0.8227	0.7921
5	0.9515	0.9057	0.8626	0.8219	0.7835	0.7473
6	0.9420	0.8880	0.8375	0.7903	0.7462	0.7050
7	0.9327	0.8706	0.8131	0.7599	0.7107	0.6651
8	0.9235	0.8535	0.7894	0.7307	0.6768	0.6274
9	0.9143	0.8368	0.7664	0.7026	0.6446	0.5919
10	0.9053	0.8203	0.7441	0.6756	0.6139	0.5584
11	0.8963	0.8043	0.7224	0.6496	0.5847	0.5268
12	0.8874	0.7885	0.7014	0.6246	0.5568	0.4970
13	0.8787	0.7730	0.6810	0.6006	0.5303	0.4688
14	0.8700	0.7579	0.6611	0.5775	0.5051	0.4423
15	0.8613	0.7430	0.6419	0.5553	0.4810	0.4173
16	0.8528	0.7284	0.6232	0.5339	0.4581	0.3936
17	0.8444	0.7142	0.6050	0.5134	0.4363	0.3714
18	0.8360	0.7002	0.5874	0.4936	0.4155	0.3503
19	0.8277	0.6864	0.5703	0.4746	0.3957	0.3305
20	0.8195	0.6730	0.5537	0.4564	0.3769	0.3118
25	0.7798	0.6095	0.4776	0.3751	0.2953	0.2330
30	0.7419	0.5521	0.4120	0.3083	0.2314	0.1741
35	0.7059	0.5000	0.3554	0.2534	0.1813	0.1301
40	0.6717	0.4529	0.3066	0.2083	0.1420	0.0972
45	0.6391	0.4102	0.2644	0.1712	0.1113	0.0727
50	1.0000	0.3715	0.2281	0.1407	0.0872	0.0543

TABLE A–3 *Continued*

PERIODS	7%	8%	9%	10%	11%	12%	13%
1	0.9346	0.9259	0.9174	0.9091	0.9009	0.8929	0.8850
2	0.8734	0.8573	0.8417	0.8264	0.8116	0.7972	0.7831
3	0.8163	0.7938	0.7722	0.7513	0.7312	0.7118	0.6931
4	0.7629	0.7350	0.7084	0.6830	0.6587	0.6355	0.6133
5	0.7130	0.6806	0.6499	0.6209	0.5935	0.5674	0.5428
6	0.6663	0.6302	0.5963	0.5645	0.5346	0.5066	0.4803
7	0.6227	0.5835	0.5470	0.5132	0.4817	0.4523	0.4251
8	0.5820	0.5403	0.5019	0.4665	0.4339	0.4039	0.3762
9	0.5439	0.5002	0.4604	0.4241	0.3909	0.3606	0.3329
10	0.5083	0.4632	0.4224	0.3855	0.3522	0.3220	0.2946
11	0.4751	0.4289	0.3875	0.3505	0.3173	0.2875	0.2607
12	0.4440	0.3971	0.3555	0.3186	0.2858	0.2567	0.2307
13	0.4150	0.3677	0.3262	0.2897	0.2575	0.2292	0.2042
14	0.3878	0.3405	0.2992	0.2633	0.2320	0.2046	0.1807
15	0.3624	0.3152	0.2745	0.2394	0.2090	0.1827	0.1599
16	0.3387	0.2919	0.2519	0.2176	0.1883	0.1631	0.1415
17	0.3166	0.2703	0.2311	0.1978	0.1696	0.1456	0.1252
18	0.2959	0.2502	0.2120	0.1799	0.1528	0.1300	0.1108
19	0.2765	0.2317	0.1945	0.1635	0.1377	0.1161	0.0981
20	0.2584	0.2145	0.1784	0.1486	0.1240	0.1037	0.0868
25	0.1842	0.1460	0.1160	0.0923	0.0736	0.0588	0.0471
30	0.1314	0.0994	0.0754	0.0573	0.0437	0.0334	0.0256
35	0.0937	0.0676	0.0490	0.0356	0.0259	0.0189	0.0139
40	0.0668	0.0460	0.0318	0.0221	0.0154	0.0107	0.0075
45	0.0476	0.0313	0.0207	0.0137	0.0091	0.0061	0.0041
50	0.0339	0.0213	0.0134	0.0085	0.0054	0.0035	0.0022

T A B L E   A–3 *Concluded*

PERIODS	14%	15%	16%	17%	18%	19%	20%
1	0.8772	0.8696	0.8621	0.8547	0.8475	0.8403	0.8333
2	0.7695	0.7561	0.7432	0.7305	0.7182	0.7062	0.6944
3	0.6750	0.6575	0.6407	0.6244	0.6086	0.5934	0.5787
4	0.5921	0.5718	0.5523	0.5337	0.5158	0.4987	0.4823
5	0.5194	0.4972	0.4761	0.4561	0.4371	0.4190	0.4019
6	0.4556	0.4323	0.4104	0.3898	0.3704	0.3521	0.3349
7	0.3996	0.3759	0.3538	0.3332	0.3139	0.2959	0.2791
8	0.3506	0.3269	0.3050	0.2848	0.2660	0.2487	0.2326
9	0.3075	0.2843	0.2630	0.2434	0.2255	0.2090	0.1938
10	0.2697	0.2472	0.2267	0.2080	0.1911	0.1756	0.1615
11	0.2366	0.2149	0.1954	0.1778	0.1619	0.1476	0.1346
12	0.2076	0.1869	0.1685	0.1520	0.1372	0.1240	0.1122
13	0.1821	0.1625	0.1452	0.1299	0.1163	0.1042	0.0935
14	0.1597	0.1413	0.1252	0.1110	0.0985	0.0876	0.0779
15	0.1401	0.1229	0.1079	0.0949	0.0835	0.0736	0.0649
16	0.1229	0.1069	0.0930	0.0811	0.0708	0.0618	0.0541
17	0.1078	0.0929	0.0802	0.0693	0.0600	0.0520	0.0451
18	0.0946	0.0808	0.0691	0.0592	0.0508	0.0437	0.0376
19	0.0829	0.0703	0.0596	0.0506	0.0431	0.0367	0.0313
20	0.0728	0.0611	0.0514	0.0433	0.0365	0.0308	0.0261
25	0.0378	0.0304	0.0245	0.0197	0.0160	0.0129	0.0105
30	0.0196	0.0151	0.0116	0.0090	0.0070	0.0054	0.0042
35	0.0102	0.0075	0.0055	0.0041	0.0030	0.0023	0.0017
40	0.0053	0.0037	0.0026	0.0019	0.0013	0.0010	0.0007
45	0.0027	0.0019	0.0013	0.0009	0.0006	0.0004	0.0003
50	0.0014	0.0009	0.0006	0.0004	0.0003	0.0002	0.0001

TABLE A-4

Present Value of an Annuity of \$1
$PVIFA = (1 - 1/(1 + k)^n)/k$

PERIODS	1%	2%	3%	4%	5%	6%
1	0.9901	0.9804	0.9709	0.9615	0.9524	0.9434
2	1.9704	1.9416	1.9135	1.8861	1.8594	1.8334
3	2.9410	2.8839	2.8286	2.7751	2.7232	2.6730
4	3.9020	3.8077	3.7171	3.6299	3.5460	3.4651
5	4.8534	4.7135	4.5797	4.4518	4.3295	4.2124
6	5.7955	5.6014	5.4172	5.2421	5.0757	4.9173
7	6.7282	6.4720	6.2303	6.0021	5.7864	5.5824
8	7.6517	7.3255	7.0197	6.7327	6.4632	6.2098
9	8.5660	8.1622	7.7861	7.4353	7.1078	6.8017
10	9.4713	8.9826	8.5302	8.1109	7.7217	7.3601
11	10.3676	9.7868	9.2526	8.7605	8.3064	7.8869
12	11.2551	10.5753	9.9540	9.3851	8.8633	8.3838
13	12.1337	11.3484	10.6350	9.9856	9.3936	8.8527
14	13.0037	12.1062	11.2961	10.5631	9.8986	9.2950
15	13.8651	12.8493	11.9379	11.1184	10.3797	9.7122
16	14.7179	13.5777	12.5611	11.6523	10.8378	10.1059
17	15.5623	14.2919	13.1661	12.1657	11.2741	10.4773
18	16.3983	14.9920	13.7535	12.6593	11.6896	10.8276
19	17.2260	15.6785	14.3238	13.1339	12.0853	11.1581
20	18.0456	16.3514	14.8775	13.5903	12.4622	11.4699
25	22.0232	19.5235	17.4131	15.6221	14.0939	12.7834
30	25.8077	22.3965	19.6004	17.2920	15.3725	13.7648
35	29.4086	24.9986	21.4872	18.6646	16.3742	14.4982
40	32.8347	27.3555	23.1148	19.7928	17.1591	15.0463
45	36.0945	29.4902	24.5187	20.7200	17.7741	15.4558
50	39.1961	31.4236	25.7298	21.4822	18.2559	15.7619

T A B L E A–4 *Continued*

PERIODS	7%	8%	9%	10%	11%	12%	13%
1	0.9346	0.9259	0.9174	0.9091	0.9009	0.8929	0.8850
2	1.8080	1.7833	1.7591	1.7355	1.7125	1.6901	1.6681
3	2.6243	2.5771	2.5313	2.4869	2.4437	2.4018	2.3612
4	3.3872	3.3121	3.2397	3.1699	3.1024	3.0373	2.9745
5	4.1002	3.9927	3.8897	3.7908	3.6959	3.6048	3.5172
6	4.7665	4.6229	4.4859	4.3553	4.2305	4.1114	3.9975
7	5.3893	5.2064	5.0330	4.8684	4.7122	4.5638	4.4226
8	5.9713	5.7466	5.5348	5.3349	5.1461	4.9676	4.7988
9	6.5152	6.2469	5.9952	5.7590	5.5370	5.3282	5.1317
10	7.0236	6.7101	6.4177	6.1446	5.8892	5.6502	5.4262
11	7.4987	7.1390	6.8052	6.4951	6.2065	5.9377	5.6869
12	7.9427	7.5361	7.1607	6.8137	6.4924	6.1944	5.9176
13	8.3577	7.9038	7.4869	7.1034	6.7499	6.4235	6.1218
14	8.7455	8.2442	7.7862	7.3667	6.9819	6.6282	6.3025
15	9.1079	8.5595	8.0607	7.6061	7.1909	6.8109	6.4624
16	9.4466	8.8514	8.3126	7.8237	7.3792	6.9740	6.6039
17	9.7632	9.1216	8.5436	8.0216	7.5488	7.1196	6.7291
18	10.0591	9.3719	8.7556	8.2014	7.7016	7.2497	6.8399
19	10.3356	9.6036	8.9501	8.3649	7.8393	7.3658	6.9380
20	10.5940	9.8181	9.1285	8.5136	7.9633	7.4694	7.0248
25	11.6536	10.6748	9.8226	9.0770	8.4217	7.8431	7.3300
30	12.4090	11.2578	10.2737	9.4269	8.6938	8.0552	7.4957
35	12.9477	11.6546	10.5668	9.6442	8.8552	8.1755	7.5856
40	13.3317	11.9246	10.7574	9.7791	8.9511	8.2438	7.6344
45	13.6055	12.1084	10.8812	9.8628	9.0079	8.2825	7.6609
50	13.8007	12.2335	10.9617	9.9148	9.0417	8.3045	7.6752

TABLE A–4 *Concluded*

PERIODS	14%	15%	16%	17%	18%	19%	20%
1	0.8772	0.8696	0.8621	0.8547	0.8475	0.8403	0.8333
2	1.6467	1.6257	1.6052	1.5852	1.5656	1.5465	1.5278
3	2.3216	2.2832	2.2459	2.2096	2.1743	2.1399	2.1065
4	2.9137	2.8550	2.7982	2.7432	2.6901	2.6386	2.5887
5	3.4331	3.3522	3.2743	3.1993	3.1272	3.0576	2.9906
6	3.8887	3.7845	3.6847	3.5892	3.4976	3.4098	3.3255
7	4.2883	4.1604	4.0386	3.9224	3.8115	3.7057	3.6046
8	4.6389	4.4873	4.3436	4.2072	4.0776	3.9544	3.8372
9	4.9464	4.7716	4.6065	4.4506	4.3030	4.1633	4.0310
10	5.2161	5.0188	4.8332	4.6586	4.4941	4.3389	4.1925
11	5.4527	5.2337	5.0286	4.8364	4.6560	4.4865	4.3271
12	5.6603	5.4206	5.1971	4.9884	4.7932	4.6105	4.4392
13	5.8424	5.5831	5.3423	5.1183	4.9095	4.7147	4.5327
14	6.0021	5.7245	5.4675	5.2293	5.0081	4.8023	4.6106
15	6.1422	5.8474	5.5755	5.3242	5.0916	4.8759	4.6755
16	6.2651	5.9542	5.6685	5.4053	5.1624	4.9377	4.7296
17	6.3729	6.0472	5.7487	5.4746	5.2223	4.9897	4.7746
18	6.4674	6.1280	5.8178	5.5339	5.2732	5.0333	4.8122
19	6.5504	6.1982	5.8775	5.5845	5.3162	5.0700	4.8435
20	6.6231	6.2593	5.9288	5.6278	5.3527	5.1009	4.8696
25	6.8729	6.4641	6.0971	5.7662	5.4669	5.1951	4.9476
30	7.0027	6.5660	6.1772	5.8294	5.5168	5.2347	4.9789
35	7.0700	6.6166	6.2153	5.8582	5.5386	5.2512	4.9915
40	7.1050	6.6418	6.2335	5.8713	5.5482	5.2582	4.9966
45	7.1232	6.6543	6.2421	5.8773	5.5523	5.2611	4.9986
50	7.1327	6.6605	6.2463	5.8801	5.5541	5.2623	4.9995

INDEX

Accrual or accretion bond, 116
Adjust the pool, 127
American Stock Exchange (AMEX), 91,
  92–97
Appearance of Impropriety, 68–69
Asset-backed
  bonds, 115
  commercial paper, 118
  preferred stock, 118
  securities, 113–147
    definition, 113
    nature, 114–115
Asset pool, 125–129
  information, 126
Authorized subsidiaries, 77

Bank Holding Company Act, 6–7
Bearer bond, 100–101
Best efforts, 3
Blue list, 70
Bond ratings, 105
Book runner, 35
Boston Co., 164–166
Bulge bracket, 39

Cap, 29
Capital Requirements, 108
Citicorp, 157–159
Collateral trust bonds, 102
Collateralized mortgage
  obligations, 143
Commercial assets, 126
Common stock, 22, 85–91
Comparison bonds, 145
Competitive bids, 53
Competitive position, 108

Consumer assets, 125
Convertible bonds, 97
Coupon rate, 49, 50
Credit enhancement, 130, 137–140
Credit enhancers, 121–122
Credit rating, 18
Credit rating agencies, 18
Credit risk, 124–126
Customer mix, 108

Debt, 20,21
Debt capacity, 20
Debt ratio, 20, 21
Deferred-interest, 104
Derivatives, 26
Deutsche Bank, 169–171
Disclosure guidelines for state
  and local government securities,
  62–65
Distribution syndicate, 38, 39.
Dreyfus Corporation, 164–166
Due diligence, 35

EBIT, 21,22
Econometric prepayment models, 142
Economics and demographics, 108
Electric Utility Bonds, 107
Equipment trust certificates, 102
Equity-related, 22
  security, 24
Excess capacity margins, 108
Exchangeable bonds, 102

Fast pay/slow pay, 139
Federal power agencies, 107

Financial guarantee from third
    parties, 122
Financial position, 108
Firm commitment, 2
Fixed rate, 24, 28
Floating rate, 24, 28, 29, 31, 103
Focus assets, 126
Fuel mix and asset concentration, 108
Full faith and credit obligations, 59

General obligation bonds, 59
Glass-Steagall Act, 3–5, 7, 8,
    10, 47, 75
Goldman Sachs case, 153–157
Guaranteed bonds, 102

Hausbank, 167

Incidental powers, 6
Industry expertise, 109
Interest-only, 145
International Connection, 169–174
Investment bankers, 121
Investment grade, 106
Investment letter, 34
Investor-owned utilities, 107
Issuer, 120, 134–137

J. P. Morgan, 10, 159–162
Junk bonds, 103

Lead manager, 35–37, 39
Letter of credit, 122
LIBOR (London Interbank Offered
    Rate), 26, 105
LO (Lease Obligations), 21

Major bracket, 39
Management fee, 40
Management focus, 108

MTN (Medium-term note), 104–105
Mellon Bank, 164– 166
Mezzanine bracket, 39
Mortgage-backed pay-through bonds,
    143–146
Mortgage bond, 101
Mortgage products, 144
Municipal bonds, 58, 59, 70–72
Municipal utilities, 107
NASD (National Association of
    Securities Dealers), 38
NASDAQ, 91, 92–97
National Bank Act, 6
NationsBank, 171–173
Noncompetitive bids, 53
Notes, 101
Notional principal amount, 28
Nuclear Exposure, 108

Offering date, 39
Off-the-run, 50
On-going disclosure, 67–68
On-the-run, 50
Opportunity cost, 27
Original maturity, 48, 49
Originators, 120, 129–131
Originator's bankruptcy, 130
Orphan subsidiary, 121

Participation certificates, 140
Pass-through securities, 114
Pay-through bonds, 115
Planned amortization classes, 144
PNC Mutual Funds, 162–164
Preferred stock, 23, 84
Premium, 29
Prepayment
    assumptions, 141
    bond, 144
    risk, 116, 141
Pricing consideration, 32
Primary Government Securities
    Dealers, 55, 56
Primary market, 50

Principal-only, 145
Private equity issues, 166–169
    confidentiality, 167
    speed, 167
    certainty, 167
    pricing, 167
    prestige, 168
Private insurance, 122
Private placement, 33
Prospectus, 35, 36
Public offering, 33, 34–35
    initial public offerings (IPO), 38
Putable bond, 103

Red herring, 36
Registered bond, 100–101
Regulatory environment, 107
Relationship banking, 18
Reserve accounts, 138
Restructuring the pool, 127
Revenue bonds, 59
Rural electric cooperatives, 107

Secondary market, 69
Securitization, 119–131
    elements, 120
Senior-subordinated structure, 122
Serial bond, 101
Servicer, 132–134, 120
Settlement frequency, 31
Shelf registration, 36, 37
Shifting interest, 139
SFP (Sinking fund payments), 22
Sinking fund provisions, 101
Spread account, 122
Stabilizing bid, 40
Standby underwriting, 2
Step-down, 139
Stop-out bid, 53
Stop-out price, 53
Straight equity, 22
Strike rate, 31
Submajor bracket, 39

Subordinated debentures, 102
Step-up bonds, 104
Swaption (Option on a swap
    contract), 28
Syndicate, 37

Tail, 54
Targeted amortization classes, 145
Tax Reform Act of 1986, 59–61
Term bonds, 101
Term of contract, 31
TIE (Times-Interest-Earned-ratio), 21
Toronto-Dominion Case, 80–83
Tranches, 116
Transfer of title, 129
True sale, 129
Trustees, 123, 137
Treasury
    auction,, 51–55
    bills, 48, 50
    bonds, 48, 50
    notes, 48, 50
    securities, 48, 49
Transfer agent, 100
Twelve year prepaid life, 141

Underlying interest rate index, 30, 31
Underwriter's spread, 2
Underwriting, 2, 41, 44, 61, 62, 83, 97
Underwriting fee, 40–41

Volatility of the index, 31

Warrants, 102

Yield curve, 31

Z-bond, 116
Zero-coupon, 103

The Bankers Guide to the Secondary Market

Securities Trading, Derivative Instruments, and Mutual Fund Services in Commercial Banking

Hazel J. Johnson, Ph.D.

This insightful guide provides an expanded knowledge of the explosive secondary market. Designed to help the reader stay ahead in today's financial services industry, *The Banker's Guide to the Secondary Market* offers a competitive edge to staying on top of the customer's changing needs.

ISBN: 1-55738-922-5 $50.00

Interest Rate Risk Management

The Banker's Guide to Using Futures, Options, Swaps, and Other Derivative Instruments

Benton E. Gup & Robert Brooks

Interest Rate Risk Management tackles this important issue, presenting simplified, nontechnical examples of how to use derivative securities to protect against swings in interest rates, explaining why some interest rates are more volatile than others. This guide includes examples for every size and every type of financial institution.

ISBN:1-55738-370-7 $65.00

Interest Rate Spreads and Market Analysis

Tools for Managing and Reducing Rate Exposure in Global Markets, Eight Edition

Citicorp

Although there has not been, and may never be, a formula to predict the future movement of interest rates and market volatility, financial managers must still contend with the pressures of investing and financing amid global market uncertainty. *Interest Rate Spreads and Market Analysis* is designed to foster an understanding of key global market rates and prices, providing a 10-year historical database for long-term and short-term indices.

ISBN: 0-78630-970-9 $65.00

Bank Mergers, Acquisitions, and Strategic Alliances

Positioning and Protecting Your Bank in the Era of Consolidation

Hazel J. Johnson, Ph.D.

Whether large or small, bankers need to assess their needs and plans for the future. Mergers and acquisitions affect every financial institution in the banking system. *Bank Mergers, Acquisitions, and Strategic Alliances in Banking* reviews the processes involved for banks facing any scenario caused by M&A activity.

ISBN: 1-55738-746-X $65.00

The Community Banker *Journal*

The Community Banker is exactly what the name suggests, a journal created for community bankers by community bankers. It spotlights a different topic in each issue that directly impacts your institution, such as branches, technology, management tools, and the people factor. *The Community Banker* tackles the strategies that are essential to staying competitive and moving ahead in today's volatile banking industry.

A Quarterly Journal by Community Bankers, for Community Bankers.
Order#CMBK $225.00 per year